DECODING TRIBAL DEVELOPMENT

Dr. KARMA LHAMU

TRANSGRESSING HOPES AND FEARS

Contents

Introduction

The development discourse has remained abstract to the 8.06% of the total Indian population comprising up of more than seven hundred and fifty scheduled tribe communities of India largely because of their voices representing their demands being left unheard by the agencies of development. The scheduled tribes are regarded to be one of the marginalized sections of society, the development of which has been tried to be addressed since the pre independence era. However, one cannot deny the fact that the desired target achievement for tribal development has not been achieved, the reasons being multiple in numbers. The forceful implementation of ideas of development as perceived by the policy formulators on the scheduled tribes without any consultation with the beneficiaries has resulted in the failure of the achievement of the desired output from the developmental policies for the scheduled tribes. The state along with the non-governmental organizations has been trying to make serious attempts to address the problems of tribal development by acting as the facilitators of development as a catalyst. The post-independence era has witnessed the implementation of a huge array of developmental policies aimed at bringing about tribal development based on the approaches designed by the first Prime Minister of independent India Pt. Nehru in close consultation with the eminent anthropologist Verrier Elwin. Elwin who was initially in favour of complete isolation was criticized by scholars like G.S. Ghurye for making an attempt to furthermore restrain the tribes backward who were referred to by Ghurye as the Backward Hindus.

Although Elwin later on changed his stand to assimilations approach, Nehru was in favour of neither complete isolation nor forceful integration of the external agencies to bring them in line with the ongoing process of development at the cost of their culture and identity. The approaches to tribal development have been witnessed to be mostly on the lines of top-down model where the policies are formulated by the government and implemented on the scheduled tribes often failing to bring about a desired result in spite of the ever increasing financial investments on the developmental plans and projects for the tribals.

The outcomes of such measures are put into question looking at the achievement of the target results. This demands for a complete re-examination of the approaches to tribal development altogether with micro level understandings in order to preserve the heterogeneous tribal identities and culture in the process of development without hampering these sensitive elements of development.

The book tries to understand the meaning of development both from the scholarly point of view as well as through the lenses of the beneficiaries themselves i.e. the scheduled tribes. The mismatch in the conceptualization of development from the two angles has stood to be one of the prime factors behind the failure of the existing policies on tribal development. Understanding the role of the third agencies of development i.e. the non-governmental organizations is also very important because in countries like India where the scheduled tribes are found to be located in the backward rural interiors, the governmental policies and their agents for the development of these communities stand to be missing due to geographical complexities. In such a situation, the non-governmental organizations are expected to cater to the needs of the tribal communities inhabiting the backward areas of the nation. However, the activities and functioning of the NGOs need to be carefully analyzed because in spite of their existence in the area for long, the goals of tribal development fail to portray a positive result.

In most of the studies the scheduled tribes have been regarded to be a homogenous single group thereby addressing their problems on a single line which has often created problem in addressing core but varied issues of the heterogenous scheduled tribes. The fact that they are composed of more than 750 different heterogeneous groups has failed to be acknowledged in the due course of policy formulations.

The detailed analysis of the major approaches from the historical point of view starting from the Anthropological approach, the British administrative approach, Political approach, Religious approach Gandhian Workers approach, Missionary approach, Assimilations Approach of Verrier Elwin, the Middle Path of Nehruvian approach etc. clearly points out towards an unaddressed existing vacuum. Due to the failure of these approaches to achieve the desired result, an alternative Structurationist Approach of Prof. Anthony Giddens has to be analysed and implemented. Giddens regards the agency and structure to be two faces of the same coin and that the line of distinction between the agency and structure is simply analytical and not distinct in nature. This is regarded to be the duality of structure of Giddens Structuration theory. He compares his idea of structuration as an orchestra where we see the presence of different instruments (agency), producing a single music (structure), yet the variations in the tone of the music produced is distinct and clear representing every instrument. In the structuration process, good and new behaviours that are beneficial to both the agency and the structure are incorporated, while the harmful and useless behaviours are patted out of the system.

The book therefore bases its reasoning on strong theoretical grounding for addressing the meaning of development in tribal context from all academic walks of life thereby opening new pathways of discussions for the much needed researches in the study area.

"There's really no such thing as the 'voiceless'. There are only the deliberately silenced, or the preferably unheard." was the remark of Arundhati Roy while receiving the 2004 Sydney Peace Prize. This deliberately unhearing the voice of the marginalized sections can be pointed out to be the main reason behind the lopsided development process. The idea of development understood to be perfectly suitable for the scheduled tribes by the policy framers and the academicians without paying heed to the perception of development of the beneficiaries themselves have flared the problem of tribal development in India. The search for the best approach for the development of the scheduled tribes has been a debatable topic for long. This is because the heterogeneity of the tribal society cannot be compromised at any cost in the name of development which in itself would stand to challenge the very idea of unity in diversity that has always stood as the binding force of India as a nation. Therefore, the idea of diversity cannot be diluted on a different scale for the marginalized communities that comprise the 8.06% of the Indian population. In this regard Amiya K. Kisku in a workshop held at the Centre for Studies of Economic Appraisal on Alternative Tribal Development Perspectives in Calcutta on March 8-10 cited in Bhaumik (1988) rightly points out that the smooth functioning of a healthy tribal lifestyle is to a major extent dependent upon a strong relationship with nature. Therefore, the problems faced by the tribals cannot be solved by the application of modern technology of development alone. This is because of their dependence upon the natural habitat and environment which demands a collaborative process of development efforts. According to Khisku, genocide and ethnocide are the two methods of decimating the tribals; genocide in the form of uprooting and displacement for giving scope to modernity and industrialization while ethnocide by the systematic destruction of tribal culture and identity.

On the other hand, we do have a school of thought that strongly disapprove the seclusion of the scheduled tribes as the specimens of study backed by the idea that these groups of people need to develop on modern lines for which a change in their culture and tradition is inevitable. Scholars like Ambika P. Ghose stand to be the vanguards of such an opinion.

Rejecting both the above stated extreme ideas of tribal development as irrelevant and unnecessary, the tribal activist such as Basta Soren cited in Bhaumik (1988) emphasizes upon the necessity to understand the internal structures of the scheduled tribe societies that act as the guiding force in their everyday life so as to bring about a serious change in the condition of the tribals. The existing culture and economy of the tribals are not taken into account in the process of development plans by the planning authorities that act as a major hindrance in the outcomes of those plans. The general idea that the tribals are helpless and backward that demands immediate guardians for help which often are found in the form of the outsider non-tribals needs to be rectified first. The concept of guardianship has always proved to be harmful for the overall development of the tribal identity which is why mere preservation of their culture and identity fail to address the mega question of tribal development. The recreation of an administrative structure by completely ignoring the existing tribal structures has proved to be a major hindrance because it is believed by scholars like Lahiri, Basu and Barman cited in Bhaumik (1988) that approximately eighty five percent of the allotted funds for tribal development are actually spent on the maintenance of the externally created administrative structure for the purpose of the supervision of the distribution of the ironically remaining ten to twenty percent of the total tribal funds to the beneficiary scheduled tribes. Therefore, the questions of the right to decide for oneself through participation of the tribals act as a major area of discussion in the due course of the studies on tribal development.

The book Decoding Tribal Development intends to delve deeper into the meaning of tribal development from both the scholarly as well as from the layman's (tribal) point of view, thereby bringing the two on a single platform of understanding in order to achieve the desired outputs from the process of development. It strives to contemplate deeper into the core understanding of development from a global to local perspective thereby locating the level of development of the heterogenous scheduled tribes of India. A detailed study of the various approaches to development has been placed alongside suggesting an alternative structurationist approach to the subject. State plays the primary role in bringing about holistic development of the nation. Therefore, a detailed list of the various programmes undertaken by the State and the government for upgrading the status of the tribes of India through diverse five-year plans and policies have been listed out in the book. Since the state alone cannot bring about the desired results, the role of the other agencies of development such as the non-governmental organizations and the civil societies have been elaborated.

The book strives to act as a vanguard in opening up new ways of understanding tribal development through a change in lenses by viewing it not just as a universe of study but instead as the agency of development as a whole in themselves through participatory approach in major decision makings. It paves way for academicians and research scholars to conduct meaningful researches in the near future where the grim wall of segregation between the beneficiaries and the benefactors are broken off into the freedom of self-reliance.

CHAPTER ONE

Development: Conceptual Clarification

The idea of development which is generally equated to the process of transformation from savagery to civilization in all walks of life engulfing quantitative to qualitative betterment is both inevitable and desirable. It involves a holistic approach that cannot be confined to a single variable such as economy or polity. However, the change in one variable definitely leads to the change in other variables. The connotation of economic growth which was equated to development in the first phase of the development of the Development Theory has been gradually replaced by changes in the quality of human life which involves the granting of freedom to the individuals so that they may choose the best for themselves in the process of development. Apart from these, the other important elements such as environmental development, capacity building, equitable distribution of wealth, welfare based development and sustainable development, are considered to be generated as vectors of economic growth that occupy a place of strategic significance in the understanding of development. In such a situation, it is believed that the demands of the people are met with meaningful policies by the agencies of development that attempt to bring about a qualitative change in the lives of those beneficiaries for whom developmental goals are actually designed for. In the contemporary era, development is considered to be an internal social process taking place within every country, where the basic requirements of the people are fulfilled by the wise and durable application of the country's resources. Economically, the definition of development suggests the nation's fulfillment of people's needs, employment, and the improvement of national wealth. As a matter of fact, "Development Theory by itself has little value unless it is applied, unless it translates into results, and unless it improves people's lives" (Lewis T. Preston, Former President, World Bank, quoted in Todaro 2000). According to Bjorn Hettne (2009), 'Development in the modern sense implies intentional social change in accordance with societal objectives' Pointing out the fact that not all societal objectives are developmental where some are only inclined towards establishing authority, Jan Nederveen Pieterse (2012) goes a step ahead and defines development as 'the organized intervention in collective affairs according to a standard of improvement.'

Therefore, the process of development is expected to be meaningful only when it becomes reliable enough to bring about a positive qualitative change in the lives of the people which is why the interpretation of development solely on the basis of the calculation of Gross Domestic Product (GDP) or Per Capita Income stands to be questionable without fulfilling the qualitative criteria of Human Development Index (HDI). In understanding the idea of development, one cannot ignore the human factor in it because ultimately the answer to the vital question of development for whom cannot be substantiated by the mere growth in investments, infrastructures and institutional betterment without addressing the people for whom these growths are actually intended to serve. However, one cannot ignore the importance of economic growth because the definition of development to a developing nation cannot be visualized without economic betterment where poverty is seen to be a wide spread disease that can be controlled by economic betterment and later on completely cured by qualitative development. This ambitious goal of qualitative betterment must not simply try to clone the developed North, and hence should not be based on the lines of modernization alone because without addressing the core areas of development of one particular country, the superstructure created by imitating the West shall prove to be faulty in the long run. Therefore, the policy of development must be designed only after understanding, analyzing and incorporating the ideas of the people of the area that requires the intervention of the developmental agencies in bringing about development. The idea of participation of the beneficiaries hence becomes one of the primary criteria that need to be fulfilled in the formulation, implementation and analysis of the development process.

The State is the primary agency of development especially in the developing nations. It is the State that decides on the primary issues of policy formulation, implementation and the overall analysis of the success or failure of the formulated policies for bringing about development. In India, due to the adoption of a welfare model of governance, it becomes the primary responsibility of the State to cater to the needs of the common people. The ultimate target revolves around the welfare of the masses. However, there is a wide range of varieties that is engulfed in the term masses demarcated by racial affinities, caste identities, religious factionalism, communal orientations, linguistic diaspora and ethnic realism, all of which are strongly tied down into either the wealthy section or the common masses. The policy of development is generally targeted towards the upliftment of the common masses where poverty, subjugated quality of human life, violation of human rights, violence and ill health has become an integral part of their living. One such vulnerable communities of India that require a special care happens to be the scheduled tribe population that comprise 8.06% of the total population of India. Right from the pre independence era, special measures have been taken up categorizing them as a special group of the Indian population. This was followed by the Five Year Plans that have allotted special economic investments to bring about development of the scheduled tribe communities. The approach adopted in the process of tribal development in India has been derived from the Nehruvian model of middle path of neither complete isolation nor excessive intervention that which was designed almost seven decades ago. However, what was perceived by the policy framers as development was actually a reflection of an attempt to bring about modernization of the scheduled tribe communities that completely devalued their ethnic indigenous knowledge, culture, leadership and overall lifestyle. The backlash of this attempt of faulty approach and modernization is clearly seen in the failure of the policies and programmes devised by the intellectual elites for the backward and poor scheduled tribes without taking into consideration their needs, aspirations, beliefs and choices. Such a result is not just a shock in itself but a lesson too because history stands as a testament to the failure of any policy that ignores the opinions of the beneficiaries to which tribal development is not an exception to.

While advocating the meaning of development, one needs to address its goals first. Without a vision, the planning and execution of such plans stand to be faulty like the one that has been reflected in the case of tribal development in India. Due to the development in technology, the world today is conceived as a global village where a development of any form be it political, economic or social in any part of the globe is likely to affect the other. In such a situation, the dream of developing all the parts of the globe stands to be important. The United Nations Organization has played an important role in helping the exchange of ideas of development for which there have taken special efforts in keeping track of the scale of development of every country, especially the developing ones. The realization that without the freedom to decide for one's own destiny, development cannot be imposed upon by external intervention. The United Nation Organization in its Vienna Declaration commonly referred to as Right to Development (RTD) as a Human Right, regards this freedom to be fundamental in bringing about qualitative change in the lives of the people. The seventeen Sustainable Developmental Goals (SDGs) commonly referred to as Envision 2030 engulfing the visions of 'No Poverty, Zero Hunger, Good Health and well Being, Quality Education, Gender Equality, Clean Water and Sanitation, Affordable and Clean Energy, Decent Work and economic Growth, Industry, Innovation and Infrastructure, Reduced Inequalities, Sustainable Cities and Communities, Responsible Consumption and Production, Climate Action, Life Below Water, Life on Land, Peace Justice and Strong Institutions and Partnership for the Goals.' (www.undp.org) is expected to act as a development target for every developing country in bringing about development of their countrymen. Tribal development must also be formulated on such global guidelines, not to forget the consultation of the beneficiaries themselves, in order to bring about a global development in the lives of the micro ethnic communities.

In fulfilling this target, the role of the State stands to be very important. However, after the 1990s', with the adoption of the policy of Liberalization, Privatization and Globalization, and Laissez faire or economic freedom, the role of the State was virtually curtailed. The vacuum created was therefore filled in by the third sectors of development commonly referred to as the non-governmental organizations. The primary aim of such organizations was to work on the implementation of the formulated policies of the government in order to bring about the development of the common people. The most important reasons for allowing the non-governmental organizations to fill in the vacuum not only in India but on a global platform was because of its people friendly approach, voluntary nature, grassroot mobilization and the capability to touch on the lives of the needy so that the people could look up to them in the hour of need, that which the bureaucrats were largely failing on. Depending upon the type of functioning, the non-governmental organizations are categorized into some major groups such as the Human Right NGOs, Environmental NGOs, Rights Based NGOs and Developmental NGOs. With regard to the tribal development, the developmental NGOs have an important role to play in bringing about empowerment of the beneficiaries. The role of the non-governmental organizations in the welfare and development of the tribal communities is very interesting to assert because the time span of the intervention of such non-governmental organizations has now been a long run phenomenon. This definitely demands them to be accountable for their activities in the betterment of the beneficiaries.

Tribal development as a study has now occupied a place of significance because of the plethora of events taking place, affecting the everyday lives of the scheduled tribes that have drawn the attention of the academicians from all across the globe. Due to the rise in the growth of infrastructures that is perceived as development for the masses at the cost of the livelihoods of the minority scheduled tribes leaving them alone to face the problems of displacement, exploitation, inhuman living, trafficking, poverty, ill health, mal nutrition and dejection, the condition of the tribal communities has worsened in most of the cases. In such a situation a close examination at a micro scale is very important not only about those scheduled tribes who are displaced, but on the other hand the condition of the other tribal communities under normal circumstances as well, who are not free from exploitation, poverty and dejection. An overall assessment of the socio-economic condition of the scheduled tribe communities of India does not provide us with a healthy picture. Very often, due to the negligence on the part of the developmental agencies to treat them as respectable human beings has triggered violent acts of protests, movements and terrorism. In order to avoid such untoward incidents, it is important that the underdeveloped scheduled tribe communities be studied from their lenses and their core questions of development be addressed with the help of participatory developmental approach.

The study of tribal development in India post 1990s demands a serious understanding of the interrelated index terms and its dimensions from all possible dynamics of interpretations. One cannot visualize the problem area without having a sound knowledge about the core issues of development, the changing role of the State in Development, the meaning of tribal development in India, the relevance of the Right to Development as a Human Right, and the

Role of the non-governmental organizations in the empowerment of the scheduled tribe populations.

1.1 UNDERSTANDING DEVELOPMENT

The idea of development is multidimensional in nature that cannot be confined to economic growth alone, but on the other hand addressing the humane factor / human development stands to be of equal importance. Although economic growth is a primary component of development, yet the other variables such as social upliftment, political betterment and overall empowerment in a holistic manner cannot be ignored as well. When we address the idea of development, the question for whom and how provides us with the ultimate answer to the inner meaning of this mega term because development of one variable has a definite impact upon the development of the other. It simply lies upon one's prioritization of ideas that likewise lay emphasis on the core elements of development accordingly. The lense of viewing the subject provides us with the framework where in the variables are categorized according to ones needs. However, in simplifying this prioritization process one cannot underestimate the changing phases of development paradigm that has assigned a unique position to each variable according to the need of the hour, with its core always revolving around the economic dimensions. The western model of modernization was proposed for and implemented on the poor countries after the era of decolonization which was followed by the Basic Needs Approach and then the Participatory Development Approach. Culture was not left behind because it reflected one's identity. Therefore, a special phase was dedicated to the Culture and Development Approach.

However, the major focus of attention after witnessing the depletion of natural resources as a result of excessive exploitation of nature was laid upon Sustainable Model of Development. The present era is seen to highlight upon the wellbeing and happiness of the citizens as an important variable of societal development goal.

The conceptualization and significance of development has witnessed a constant change with the passage of time. The idea of economic growth-oriented development has now been clubbed together with the human factor in it. Scholars like Mahbub Ul Haq (1996) strongly advocate the inclusion of the human aspect to development as in better standard of living, betterment of the opportunities to a good living, freedom to choose the life which one values, the granting of the exercise of human rights and not to forget the implementation of the right to development as human right. The understanding of development has shifted its focus from the study of the Per Capita Income to the Human Development Index (HDI). Therefore, the crux of development has transcended from economic growth to welfare policies. This obviously did take a long span of time to evolve which was followed by the formation of international peace keeping and developmental organizations such as the United Nations Organization, the World Bank and many such international bodies. After the end of the Second World War, the globe has witnessed a phenomenal growth in the development discourse that affected almost all the philosophy based subjects especially with the acceptance of the notion of the evolutionary stages of development standing parallel to the conceptualization of society from the barbaric age to the age of civilization. Development was therefore viewed by scholars like Iqbal Narain (1989) as something both inevitable and desirable. The idea of development in the social interpretation of the betterment of social life is a process marked by continuous growth bearing its origin to the framework of western thinking making it completely ethnocentric in its base. Mention must be made about prominent scholars such as Spencer, Durkheim, Tonnies, Morgan, who have extensively contributed to the development of this unique concept.

The post war era witnessed a sharp turn towards a welfare model of development where culture was regarded to be an integral part to it. This was seconded by the active participation and the strong international vigil of the UNO. The historic declaration of the mighty body in understanding and making the member countries understand the significance of world peace, harmony and brotherhood by welfare policies can be regarded to be the guide for all such actions towards human development. It was then that eminent scholars like Paulo Freire (1970) who strongly advocated for participatory model of development where the local problem would be selected and addressed to by the local people. They were against the idea of top to bottom trickle-down approach.

The United Nations in its first proposal for action of 1960-70 also considered as the development decade stated that development should be understood as growth along with change in all aspects of human life i.e. social, cultural, qualitative and quantitative with its key element resting on the improvement of the quality of the life of the people. The Declaration of Cocoyoc of 1974 emphasized on the development of human beings and not of things thereby stressing on the need for diversity for following different roles to achieve the goal of self-reliance in the process of development. UNEP–UNCTAD (1974).

In 1975, the UNESCO propagated human centred development with its emphasis on the multi relational process that includes all aspects of the life of collectivism, of its relationship with the outside world and of its own consciousness. UNESCO (1977).

Development today has occupied the base line of all modern thinking in the contemporary era be it in the field of science, technology, ethics, values, social organization and democracy that has been fused into the ultimate aim of producing a better world. 'In its strong sense, development means using the productive resources of society to improve the living conditions of the poorest people. In its weaker sense, development means more of everything for everyone in the context of a lot more for a few; which in itself is expected to take place through the trickle-down process adopted in the developmental approach.' Peet and Hartwick (2005).

Although economic independence is definitely the core of development yet the narrow meaning of development as economic growth and expansion has been extended to incorporate the widening choices of people as a fundamental freedom in order to fulfil the criteria of basic human rights. In doing so the human development factor has added more meaning to this multidimensional interpretation of development. Human development refers to the extension of the choices of the people that help in their enhancement of capabilities and functioning that require technological betterment, social upgradation along with the improvement of creativity in human beings. The achievement of these qualities will definitely result in economic growth but here as well one cannot equate the growth of gross domestic product (GDP) with the expansion of capabilities. Griffin and Knight (1990) regard these two areas as closely linked but not identical. The only point of difference here lies in one's interpretation about the importance of one variable that determines the other. In the earlier records, it was believed that economic growth would directly or indirectly lead to the enhancement of capabilities. However, in the contemporary era it is the opposite in reality. Opinions have been raised stating that the betterment in the capabilities of individuals with the help of extension of freedom directly or indirectly leads to economic growth.

According to the UNDP, "Human Development is a development paradigm that is about much more than the rise or fall of national income. It is about creating an environment in which people can develop their full potential and lead productive, creative lives in accord with their needs and interests. People are the real wealth of nations. Development is thus about expanding the choices people have to lead lives that they value. And it is thus about much more than economic growth, which is only a means – it a very important one – of enlarging people's choices." (www.hdr.undp.org/en/humandev). Griffin (2006) explains it further by stating that the above mentioned idea of the UNDP cannot be equated to a formula that can be mechanically applied, but on the other hand it contains those ingredients that distinguish it from commodity centred approaches to development.

1.2 DEFINING DEVELOPMENT

In the terms of the British Dictionary, development is defined as the process in which someone or something grows or changes and *becomes more advanced*. The Business Dictionary furthermore adds to it by defining it as the process of economic and social transformation that is based on complex cultural and environmental factors and their interactions. (www.dictionary.cambridge.org).

Development aims to bring about betterment from a single humanitarian perspective by incorporating the modern advances made in the fields of science, technology, democracy, values, ethics and social organization. Development therefore denotes the utilization of the productive resources of society for the improvement of the condition of the poor. On a less significant note, development means 'more of everything for everyone in the context of a lot more for a few.' Peet (2005).

Development in general terms means the use of productive resources of society to improve the living conditions of the poorest people. In its loose sense, development means a more of everything for everyone in the context of lot more for a few. Peet, R. (2005). Though economic growth is an important component of development, yet it cannot be taken to be the whole of it. Other aspects such as human development, environmental development, capacity building and sustainable development, welfare based development and equitable distribution of wealth all of which are generated as the vectors of economic growth occupy a place of strategic significance in the understanding of the concept of development. Stemming from enlightenment notions of the use of the modern scientific mind for improving existence, development entails human emancipation in two senses: a) liberation from the vicissitudes of nature through advanced technology and b) self – emancipation i.e. control over social relations, conscious control over the conditions under which human nature is formed. In both the senses development refers to economic, social and cultural progress including finer ethical ideals and higher moral values. In other words, development means the improvement of the complexly interlinked nature, economy, society, culture and political conditions.

According to Anand Kashyap (1998), Development of a society instead of being a monolithic and linear process of creating economic abundance is a holistic process of social transformation from less creative to greater creative participation of its members at the individual and collective levels. Emphasis on creative participation implies minimization of disorderliness in social system and maximization of creativity so as to achieve a symbiotic transformation of *man- nature and society relationship.*

Development is considered to be an internal, social process taking place within every country, where the basic requirements of the people are fulfilled by the wise and durable application of the country's resources. Economically, the definition of development suggests the nation's fulfilment of people's needs, employment, and the improvement of national wealth. As a matter of fact, "Development Theory by itself has little value unless it is applied, unless it translates into results, and unless it improves people's lives" (Lewis T. Preston, Former President, World Bank, Quoted in Todaro 2000). The Positivist school of thought begins with the understanding of the concept of development as something closely related to "Value Judgment". Very often the idea of development is regarded to be a normative issue, a synonym for improvement.

Using the Marxian Analysis, one can regard economic development to be the base of all forms of development. Hence, the focal point of economic development is the economic condition of developing countries regarding economic matters and the development of policies that improve a nation's position economically, socially and institutionally.

Consequently, social, economic and political aspects are included in theories of economic development, which apply different models related to different key concepts (Martinussen 1997; Roberts and Hite 2000).

Several definitions exist for development and offer different focal concepts. For instance, Modernisation Theory stresses the cultural features of each society, such as political, religion and culture. On the other hand, World Systems Theory and Globalisation seek to evaluate external relationships and to define different points in the development of countries.

1.3 GROWTH AND DEVELOPMENT

It is seen that generally the term growth and development are used interchangeably. Simply bringing about growth in terms of the economic achievements does not qualify itself to be termed as development because there is a thin line of demarcation between growth and development. Growth is a short term as well as a narrow concept which only looks upon the figurative assumptions deciding on the level of betterment of human beings only on the calculations of Gross Domestic Product and Gross National Product by tabulating the Per Income Capita of the people. In doing so, it fails to look into the human aspect of development because the ultimate question to be answered here is development for whom? The obvious answer to this inquiry would be the development or the betterment of the lifestyle of the people. Technically, development differs from economic growth in the sense that development lays emphasis on the condition of production and the betterment of this condition. The condition referred to means the environment affected by the economic activity affecting up to the social consequences like income distribution and human welfare. On the other hand, growth in general and economic growth in particular emphasizes on the increase of economic productivity. Development indicates betterment/ transformation or improvement of working condition while growth refers to increasing the size or getting bigger. While development incorporates physical, social as well as psychological change, growth includes only physical change. Similarly, while development indicates both qualitative as well as quantitative transformations, growth generally indicates only the quantitative transformations. Therefore, it can be stated that development affects the skill, values, human capabilities, and the human behavioural pattern towards betterment. There are different types of growth out of which economic growth stands to be significant. Economic growth and economic development are interrelated. The rise in the Gross Domestic Product of a country symbolizes a rise in the economic growth. The tools to measure the economic development of a country are the life expectancy rate, infant morbidity rate, poverty rate, literacy rate and the overall health condition level. Therefore, it becomes clear from the above given compartmentalization that for assessing the improvement of any nation, emphasis must be laid on holistic development and not on growth alone.

Development advocates human emancipation in two ways. The first one being freedom from the miseries of nature with the help of advanced technology and the second one being self emancipation which means control over social relations so as to achieve a controlled human nature. Development therefore stands for the overall improvement of the complexly inter linked areas such as human nature, economy, society, culture and political conditions. On the other hand, developmentalism means the faith or the belief in the possibility and the desirability of the above discussed method of economic progress. (Richard Peet in his book Theories of Development argues that development is a complex contradictory phenomenon.)

The measurement of development in the capitalist society is conventionally done purely on the size of the economy by looking at the Gross National Product (GNP) i.e. "the total final output of goods and services produced by an economy". (World Bank 1989:291)- Where the higher the growth of GNP, the more rapidly a country is assumed to develop. An alternative measure that takes into account and emphasizes on the cultural and social dimensions as equally important to the economic aspect is the Human Development Index (HDI). The HDI is calculated by the United Nations Development Programme (UNDP). The HDI takes into account the development variables such as access to knowledge, nutrition and health services, leisure hour, security, political and cultural freedoms, life expectancy at birth, adult literacy rate, income sufficiency rate etc which helps in understanding the level of development as a social progress. In order to assess the different dimensions of human development, the UNDP also calculates the "Human Freedom Index" (HFI) that measures the rule of law, political participation, non discrimination and freedom of expression. Therefore, Development occupies a holistic understanding as compared to growth because development cannot be studied as a one-dimensional concept. It is an interrelated idea which has its strong base in the economic, social and political dynamics of life.

1.4 OUTLINING A BRIEF HISTORY OF DEVELOPMENT

The phenomenal growth of the development theory is a phenomenon of the post Second World War period although its inception can be seen in the ancient sociological as well as anthropological studies. Dube (1989) has pointed out four distinct phases of the development studies. In the *first phase* the meaning of development was confined to economic development alone where the focus of attention was on economic growth, capital formation and the growth in infrastructures. However, this was challenged when the impact of this growth rate did not match the distribution of the surplus amongst the deserving which was completely left to trickle-down process that was slow and none egalitarian in nature. The *second phase* was marked by the relationship between economic development and social change. It was believed that the institutional factors hindered economic development and technical change for which the modification of the institutional framework of the society would definitely accelerate the process of economic development. This phase gave birth to the modernization paradigm where scholars resorted to case studies in pointing out the hindrances created by the institutional structures which needed alteration following the development model generally of the West. The *third phase* represented a strong reaction against the insufficient earlier paradigms of modernization and development which is why it has been described as the reactive and responsive phase. It aimed to find out the key to successful praxis of development by stating that the faulty institutional structures cannot be regarded as the sole responsible factor behind the underdevelopment, dependency and neo-colonialism. Therefore, a call for better access of common men to the planning process in bringing about human centred development was highlighted. The *fourth phase* is also regarded to be reflective phase where equal emphasis was to be given to both the national and international order with the formation of a New International Economic Order (NIEO) for the development of the developed, developing and the underdeveloped.

As has been stated above, the historical understanding of the source of development stands to be multifaceted. However, many scholars are of the opinion that intellectual understanding of development can be traced to the European Enlightenment of the eighteenth century that is characterized by progress, modernity and rationalism. The modern day thinking about development revolves around the core concept of economic growth. With the passage of time mechanization and industrialization became an integral part of development which therefore broadened its meaning to encompass the idea of modernization. Here economic growth was in paralleled with political modernization engulfing in itself nation building alongside social modernization developing entrepreneurship and target achievement orientation. This was followed by the dependency theory where capital accumulation and economic growth occupied the centre stage which was followed by the other dimension of dependency that led to a large scale development of underdevelopment i.e. increase in the number of dependent bodies. The alternative understanding of development which was proposed later on was on the focus of community development, social development and in turn human development. The idea of 'human flourishing' which had a strong hold in the 1980s relied largely on Amartya Sens works on capacities and entitlements that ultimately implied the development of human capacities. The central idea of development in the Human Development Report of the United Nations Development Programme is the 'enlargement of people's choice'. Pieterse (2010).

Around the same time, two major radically different perspectives on development emerged. The first being the *neoliberals* who disregard the developing economies to be a special case. The disorders in economic terms must be done away with only by the market forces and no other agencies like the government should intervene in fixing up the problems of the developing economies which otherwise would lead to market distortion. Instead, the ultimate aim of economic growth must be achieved through deregulation, liberalization and privatization. Therefore, the agency of development change hands from the State to the market. 'Accordingly, neo liberalism is an anti-development perspective.' Pieterse (2010). The perspective was that propounded by the *post development* thinkers. They also propagate the 'anti-development' perspective in the sense that they accuse the state of possessing authoritarian mechanism which lead to the repudiation of economic goal and therefore ultimately results in the disaster of the majority population. (Rahnema and Bawtree 1997)

The chronological understanding of development is that of a mixed one. It starts with the application of science and technology to the collective organization and also tries to manage the changes that arise out of the application of science and technology. Virtually from the outset development ranges from infrastructural works to industrial policies, welfare state, new economic policies, colonial economics and ultimately Keynesian demand management. This implies that there are different connotations to the understanding of the term development. The first is to look at it as a part of the development critique i.e. deconstruction of development. The second is to treat it as a part of the historical context carrying a different meaning under different circumstances, thereby serving as a reflective mirror under different situations.

Tracing the history of development, Paul Hopper (2012) in his mega work Understanding Development Issues and Debates, has categorized the issue into six phases. These can be listed as follows:

1940s and 1950s

The development of the idea of development started after the Second World War with the creation of the United Nations Organizations with specialized agencies like the International Monetary Fund and the World Bank that were specially crafted to enhance post war reconstruction and the economic stability at the international forum. It must be noted here that the approaches and policies of development that were applied in the 1940s and 1950s were in fact already outlined in the 1920s and the 1930s which remained unimplemented due to the Great Depression and the Second World War. Some even trace the origin of developmental practice to the colonial era precisely to the passing of the Colonial Development Act 1929 and the setting up of the Colonial Development Fund where small amount of British funds were distributed among the colonies for the purpose of economic development. Similar activities also took place in France in a parallel fashion. However, some scholars like Uma Kothari (2001) stand sceptical to the claims made by the imperialist countries about the efforts of economic development in the colonies. In tracing the relationship between colonialism and development, various motives stand out to be pertinent out of which two are very much prominent. The *first* one being that the outwardly efforts of economic development brought about by the developed nations on the colonies were actually an effort to make the latter the partners of trade which would in turn enhance the economy of the former and not the latter. *Secondly*, countries like Britain and France by using such policies were in fact trying to veil themselves as benevolent powers to surpass the international criticisms against the practice of colonialism which was viewed as an exploitative, extractive and a questionable practice.

1960s

The 1960s were defined by the modernization theories that were clubbed together by the writings of prominent scholars of the South such as Samir Amin (1976), Andre Gunder Frank (1996) and Arghiri Emmanuel (1974) all of who criticized the fact that the economic growth had failed to materialize the countries who were witnessing economic growth including the South. They advocated about the unfair terms of trade between the North and the South and also the dependency that had been generated where the South became dependent over the North in terms of international economic relations.

1970s

1970s witnessed the strengthening of the dependency theory due to the deepening of global inequalities. International agencies like the

World Bank and the International Labour Organization focused on the vital issues such as 'redistribution with growth' and 'basic needs', thereby catering towards the need of the poor. This decade also witnessed a change in the focal point from growth towards the role of gender equality in development. Alongside it also emphasized on the growing environmental awareness as that propagated in the UN Stockholm Conference on the human Environment.

1980s

The remarkable feature witnessed in the 1980s was the debt crisis faced by the developing countries specifically Africa and Latin America facing a decline in the Foreign Direct Investment (FDI) due to the unfavourable lending conditions in the international scenario. Many of the developing countries sought to financial assistance from the international organizations such as the IMF and the World Bank. The statist theories of development received a jolt due to the collapse of the socialist states in Eastern Europe leading to the development of neo liberalism in the main line orientation of development. This was verified by the fact that SAPs (Structural Adjustment Programmes) or the financial assistance programmes for the developing countries was conditioned upon the fact of participation in the global markets. The concept of sustainable development also received increased acceptance in the developmental circles in this decade which was guaranteed by the holding of the World commission on Environment and Development and the drafting of the famous chapter nine i.e. Our Common Future in the Brundtland Report.

1990s

In this decade, alongside the neo liberal perspective to development orientation, the post development dynamics entered the stage which very much questioned the former. The major focus of attention was shifted to culture and indigenous knowledge. "Indeed, culture became an increasingly important theme within development." Schech and Haggis (2000). Parallel to this event, the fossil fuel driven economic growth in China and India was also on the rise. The signing of the Kyoto Accord 1997 testified the rising significance of environmental conservation under the aegis of development dynamics. Due to the widespread criticism of the SAPs, the employment of local vocabulary and participation of the local people for poverty reduction was implemented. "This shift was reflected in the World Bank's promotion of Poverty Reduction Strategies (PRSs), which places the onus upon developing countries themselves formulating their own development approaches based on local consultation. Hopper, (2012).

2000 and Onwards

With the passage of time and the changes witnessed in the understanding of development, the meaning of development today stands to accommodate in it the major ideas like neo liberalism, participatory approaches, post development perspectives and sustainable development in order to fit in the context of rapid population growth in the world form, day to day environmental degradation and globalization. These are aided by the issues and debates on international trade terms, debts, role of foreign aids, good governance, human security and environmental conservation. In this regard, it is extremely essential to understand the conceptualization of development from the stand point of the United Nations Organisation. This is because the UN provides the institutional framework within which the contemporary debate on development takes place. The United Nations was created to in the aftermath of the Second World War in order to address the development and other related issues. In doing this, various minor organizations under the banner of the United Nations Organisations were brought into existence to cater to the in detail micro developmental aspects.

1.5 CORE COMPONENTS OF DEVELOPMENT

The understanding of development demands the embracing of the major socio-economic objectives and values that is strived for in a society. Goulet in 1971 made an extra ordinary attempt to distinguish the three basic core values or the core components in extracting the wider meaning of development. These core elements are: life – sustenance, self esteem and freedom which can be elaborated as follows-

- ❖ **Life- Sustenance**: The provision of the basic needs for the sustenance of human life is very much essential to bring about development. The basic needs approach to development was initiated in the 1970s by the World Bank. A country cannot claim to be developed if it fails to provide to all its citizens the basic needs such as food, housing, clothing and minimum education. Therefore, the major objective of development must be to eradicate primary poverty and raising the standard of their living by providing the basic needs to them.

- **Self- Esteem**: This basically points out to the exercise and enjoyment by the people the feeling of self respect and independence. The prevalence of exploitative relationship in a country cannot boast itself of being developed. Goulet is of the opinion that the developing countries seek development for the enhancement of self esteem, the eradication of the feeling of dependence and dominance that is generally associated with an inferior economic status.

- **Freedom**: The idea of freedom here means the liberation from the evils of 'want, ignorance and squalor' which will thereby enable the people to choose their own future that they value. A person cannot be considered to be free if he is debarred from the right to choose which in turn is affected by the level of education and the skills imparted upon him.

It is to be noted here that all the three core elements are inter related. "The lack of self esteem and freedom result from low levels of life sustenance, and both lack of self esteem and economic imprisonment become links in a circular, self perpetuating chain of poverty by producing a sense of fatalism and acceptance of the established order – as what Galbraith (1980) calls it the accommodation to poverty." Thirlwall (1999).

The economic development must be expressed in terms of the expansion of the capabilities and the entitlements. It is to be noted that although for most of the people entitlement depends on their ability to sell their labour and on the price of the commodities, yet besides the market mechanism the power relationship existing in the society is one such pertinent factor that affects the due entitlement of an individual.

1.6 DEVELOPMENT AND RIGHT TO DEVELOPMENT

Development refers to the improvement in a country's economic and social conditions in way of managing an area's natural and human resources with the aim of creating wealth and improving people's lives. Dudley Seers (1969), while elaborating on the meaning of development suggests that while there can be value judgments on what is development and what is not, it should be a universally acceptable aim of development to make for conditions that lead to a realization of the potentials of human personality. Development is a concept and multi-facetted phenomena. Although, its history goes back to the antiquities, development occupied an exceptional position after the Second World War in the late 1940s. Since then, there have been efforts for social, political and economic progress all over the world facilitated by the quick technological evolution.

However, development should not be confused with growth. Development differs from economic growth in the sense that development lays emphasis on the condition of production and the betterment of this condition. Brookfield in the year 1975 defined development from a very basic level as 'change'. Robert Chambers (1997) adds to it as 'good change'. The debate between good change and bad change remains open for discussion but the major issue to be discussed here is what Cowen and Shenton (1996) have noted on 'What is intended by Development? 'However, in analyzing this question it must be noted that with the passage of time, the concept of development has accrued many different theories, approaches and interests thereby making it a multifaceted phenomenon, not only confining itself to the developing countries, but the geographical areas of the South in comparison to the North. The changing meaning and nature of development over the passage of time has furthermore complicated the conceptualization of the subject. Originally, the idea of development has emerged primarily from economic growth which gradually incorporated the quality of human life, social welfare, political freedom and the enhancement of human capacities in it. "Reflecting these changes, from the late 1980s onwards the United Nations Development Programme (UNDP) began to employ the Human Development Index (HDI) as an alternative measure of development to GDP. This is encapsulated in the 2000/2001 Human development Report (UNDP2001)." Hopper (2012). From this perspective, development means 'expanding the choices people have to lead lives they value' (UNDP 2001:9). The HDI therefore focuses upon the wellbeing of human life by the enhancement of the human capacities by providing better education and a decent standard of living. In his influential book *Development as Freedom*, Amartya Sen (1999) orients development towards enhancing the freedom of human by providing them the choice of opportunities, entitlements and capabilities.

In the conceptualization of development, one must also lay emphasis on the complexities of development. The factors that shape the course of development over a period of time stand out to be as follows- the degree of political stability and social cohesion in the country, the influence of culture and history, the natural resource endowment. Cowen and Shenton (1996) have noted that development 'comes to be defined in a multiplicity of ways because there is multiplicity of "developers" who are entrusted with the task of development. Allen, T. & Allan, T. (2000) has expressed concern that development is increasingly viewed as the practice of development agencies like multilateral organizations, governments, NGOs and social movements that conceptualize development in terms of alleviating problems and setting targets (Ibid:774). Salil Shetty, the Secretary General of Amnesty International has argued that 'we are faced with the contradiction of governments continuing to "violate the human rights of the same people whose lives they have committed to improving under the UN MDG framework". Kelly (2001). Shetty believes that the MDGs and development need to be based upon the principles of accountability and enforceability rather than simply being target oriented.

The Declaration on the Right to Development defines development as a "comprehensive economic, social, cultural and political process, which aims at the constant improvement of the wellbeing of the entire population and of all individuals, on the basis of their active, free and meaningful participation in development and in the fair distribution of benefits resulting therefrom." The process of development that is recognized as a human right is one "in which all human rights and fundamental freedoms can be fully realized." This definition provides us with the interpretation of development from the lenses of human rights.

In order to understand the core elements of the RTD, it is important for us to understand the inscribed articles of this mega declaration which reads out three major principles as: 'a) There is an inalienable human right that is called right to development; b) there is a particular process of economic, social, cultural and political development, in which all human rights and fundamental freedoms can be fully realized; and c) the right to development is a human right by virtue of which every human person and all peoples are entitled to participate in, contribute to and enjoy that particular process of development.' Sengupta (2014) (www.un-ilibrary.org).

Therefore, the right to development provides a vision to the goals of the development process which if successfully fulfilled can lead to the development of the people on a global platform.

1.7 CULTURE AND DEVELOPMENT

The importance of cultural development is severe in the understanding of development dynamics. The blanketing idea of modernization or westernization stands to be no longer acceptable in the polycentric globe constantly striving towards cultural identity. In such a situation, one can state that culture has taken the role of prominence in the overall conceptualization of development. Thinkers like Long and Villarreal in the year 1993 state that the cultural factor enters the development arena in a retreat like situation from the macro level structural approaches to micro level actor-oriented approach. Therefore, if priority is granted to the agencies over the structure such as the national economy and the state, the meaning of cultural actors become significant variables. The nexus between the conceptualization of culture and power stands to be very important.

In theorizing power and culture, the two major theories of power must be kept in mind. The national culture perspective which follows a deductive approach and which advocates culture to have been originated from macro social powers. On the other hand, the local culture perspective follows an inductive approach very much influenced from anthropological culturalism and populism. However, the major criticisms levied against this theory are that although it makes an attempt to explain cultural differences, it fails to address the issues such as inequality, misinterprets popular culture with tradition and also decontextualises the local culture.

The Culture and Development discourse tries to incorporate the conventional anthropological tools like the participant observation method well fitted to the development culture of projects. The attempts towards simplification by this discourse are not free from loopholes such as- it fails to de problematise development. It can be stated that in order to make development effective, one needs to make it participatory. In this context the Dutch development corporation policy document- *A World of Difference* (Ministry of Foreign Affairs1991) stated that 'culture must be the basis of sustainable development' and development must be 'embedded in culture'.

1.7.1 IMPORTANCE OF PARTICIPATION IN DEVELOPMENT

The participation of the people occupies a central place in the development think tank of the developing countries. Participation is commonly understood to mean engagement of the citizens in society and in decision making that have an impact on their lives. It is a political endeavor that challenges operation and discrimination, in particular of the poorest and most marginalized people. Participatory process enables people to see more clearly and learn from the complexity that they are living and working in. Participation makes an attempt to make the poor a part in initiatives designed for their benefit with the expectation that development projects will be more sustainable and successful with the engagement of the local population in the process of development.

"At the dawn of the 21st century, calls for more active engagement of poor people in development have come of age. Participation in development has gained a new respectability and legitimacy, and with the status of development orthodoxy." Cornwall (2005).

The advocates of Participatory Democracy state that the process of the so called normal development is characterized by biases, 'Eurocentrism and top-downism' which ultimately lead to disempowerment mainly because it sidelined the non expert local resources thereby resulting in limited benefits. As a mark of resentment, eminent scholars like Paulo Freire in the year 1970 advocated participatory action research creating a new environment for people to learn, express and achieve development. Robert Chambers argued that 'putting the last first' was necessary for rural development.

Participatory development focuses upon the grass root level of development that permits plurality of goals to be achieved as well as giving access to the local communities the right to self determinism that they require. Here, the role of the non - governmental organizations stands out to be prominent. Besides, the prominence of indigenous knowledge was also granted much more significance to by bringing it parallel to the scientific knowledge. Chambers explains that 'the essence of participatory rural appraisal is change and reversal –of role, behavior, relationship and learning. Outsiders do not dominate and lecture; they facilitate, sit down, listen and learn. Outsiders do not transfer technology; they share methods which local people can use for their own appraisal, analysis, planning, action, monitoring and evaluation. Outsiders do not impose their reality; they encourage and enable local people to express their own.' Chambers (1997).

1.8 STATE AND NGOS IN DEVELOPMENT

The publication of the monumental work of Adam Smith in1776 made it clear to all, that the most important role in the economic development of the country was not played by the state alone, by making it clear to the people the power of the "invisible hand" of the market. The Wealth of Nations strongly criticizes the role of the state in the economic development thereby allocating the status of problem to the government and solution to the market.

The discourse on development policy alongside the issue of state market interaction has posed to be a serious challenge to the academic fraternity particularly after the 1990s era that welcomed the policy of LPG in India. The major debate revolves around the questioning of the agency of development and tries to find a solution as to which agency should be held accountable for bringing about development in the area. The two contrasting stands are backed by two opposite ideas – the first one redeeming the state and its role in directing the development agenda; and the other supporting a market based economic system in tune with economic liberalization. After the report of 1997 published by the World Bank, some considerable amount of convergence has been witnessed between these two contrasting paradigms whereby the state and the market are now not regarded to be in competition with each other but rather have been portrayed as agents of development working side by side in complimentary terms for the achievement of development targets.

The state which was visualized as the conventional agent of change and development has gradually changed hands to globalization, regionalization, international intuitions and the market, who have successfully taken the lead in playing the role of development agencies. The classical understanding of development as equivalent to modernization and catching up with the west or the fairly advanced nations has also been challenged. This is because the idea of modernity has had a definite impact upon the ecological environment, local culture and cultural diversities.

The curtailment of the powers of the state was neutralized by the intervention of the non-governmental organizations in the implementation of the development policies framed by the government. In the case of India, Pandey (2008) believes that the failure of development programmes run by the governmental agencies, financial irregularities, non-compliance with the time framework, absence of coordination between the local people and the governmental agencies have been some of the primary reasons behind the alarming rate of rise in the number of the non-governmental organizations in India especially in the backward areas. This has earned a prestigious title of the third sector of development to the non-governmental organizations. In the contemporary era, the successful completion of the process of development cannot be expected without the active involvement of the NGOs in the development process. Commonly referred to as voluntary agencies, the non-governmental organizations need to re-qualify themselves in order o maintain the honour bestowed upon them as a powerful agency of development. The role of the developmental non-governmental organizations in the development of the scheduled tribes requires a complete reexamination to draw a sound conclusion which shall be taken up in the present research work.

1.9 CHANGING DIMENSIONS OF DEVELOPMENT

The classical understanding of development was equated to *growth in economic terms* i.e. the Gross National Product or per capita income. It was presumed that a progressive quantum of growth and development would succeed in bringing about socio political benefits to all the sections of the society. Over the passage of time, the idea of development has undergone distinct changes in its connotation. In India, development practices were geared towards growth and stability in the 1950s and early 1960s with the basic thrust being for industrialization, agricultural modernization and expansion of infrastructure, education and mass communication. However, the result of such an approach led to an increased level of poverty, illiteracy, ill health, class inequality, because of which the entire policy was reoriented in the 1970s to incorporate the philosophy of *social justice* in the development discourse. With the adoption of social justice a s the guiding force, emphasis was laid on the development of 'the weaker sections,' 'underprivileged,' and the 'deprived and marginalized groups' to bring them into the mainstream socio-economic developmental process. In the 1980s and 1990s the state oriented development strategies revolved around the concept of *empowerment*. This phase believed in the idea of 'sharing power' and was against the pre-existing unequal structural organization. Unlike the earlier phase where the marginalized sections were looked upon as the beneficiaries, this phase recognized the marginalized sections as 'partners of development', laying emphasis upon the idea that 'human person is the central subject of development' United Nations (1985). It is noteworthy to point out that this perspective has given recognition to the fact that 'economic development must be a means to bring about human development whereby empowerment of the people (women, the young adults, poor and other marginalized groups) has been visualized as the surest strategy to contribute to economic growth and thereby to social development'. United Nations (1996). The change in perspective has witnessed the incorporation of globalization in terms of structural adjustments like the reduction of state expenditure in the social sectors like health, education, food security etc and the encouragement of privatization. "Thus, the state has emerged as central to economic and social development not as direct provider of growth, but as partner, catalyst and facilitator." World Bank (1997). Thinkers like David Ray Cox & Manohar Pawar (2012) are of the view that there is a strong link between globalization and marginalization because in a free market world situation caused by globalization, the economically powerful nations tend to control the decision making capacity of the economically subordinate nations. This in turn leads to the weakening of the periphery states in the economic, cultural and political sense of the term and at the same time also leads to the fragmentation of the society due to increased inequality. In order to curb this newly created marginalization, Cox suggests the state to take charge and generate a feeling of collective identity among the citizens with the help of active civil society and effective state system.

Empowerment however does not confine itself to the mechanical process of sharing, distribution and redistribution of power but demands a drastic change in the economic, political and social set up.

Singha Roy (2001) points out that such changes should be directed towards:

- Creating new social identity of the marginalized sections in order to demolish the pre- existing unfair social order.
- Providing a required space for the expression of the opinion of the marginalized groups.
- Providing an access to knowledge, ideology and resources for their material and social wellbeing.
- Generating a social environment free from inequalities and discriminations.
- Ensuring policies towards making the marginalized people self-reliant.

Suggesting an alternative perspective to development, Jaganath Pathy (2001) is of the opinion that "there is a need to move away from the linear to the systematic model, shift from economic efficiency to *self-reliant and participatory* development, from dependencies to sustainable development through balanced interaction between nature and technology, from anthropoid – centric to ecological harmony, and finally to ensure the empowerment of social actors and groups so as to transform economic accumulation for the satisfaction of the fundamental human needs of marginalized groups." Pathy, Jaganath (2001). The alternate development model must focus in bringing about an improvement in the people's quality of life by making them self-reliant using participatory tools aimed at holistic and sustainable development.

History testifies that such changes oriented towards empowerment of the marginalize sections standing against the existing social structure succeeds only when supported by grass root mobilization, social movements, intervention of the civil societies like the Non-Governmental Organizations and well-articulated policy formulations followed by a committed and determined political execution for addressing such imbalances. In the process of bringing about development with empowerment, the role played by the government and the NGOs is very much strategic in nature. In advocating this, the India Country Paper reads out as follows- "*The nongovernmental/voluntary organizations can provide great help in this process, particularly providing the support structures needed for such groups, and associations and liaising between them and the government that both the groups and the government are sensitized to an organized approach to development*" (Ibid). Therefore, it is a matter of great interest to understand whether the institutional initiatives taken up by the state stand enough to bring about development or are the mechanisms of state simply not sufficient to empower the marginal sections. In such a situation what would be the role of the Non-Governmental Organizations in bringing about the development of the marginalize groups and what are the loopholes that need to be addressed would be an interesting area to be looked into. Mahbub Ul Haq (1996) in his work Reflections on Human Development is of the opinion that people are both the means and the end of economic development. It has been witnessed that the developmental policies of some of the societies simply based on economic terms generally do not achieve the desired output if they fail to address the vital issues such as human skills, human capital and human capabilities

Development of a society, instead of being a monolithic and a linear process of creating economic abundance, is a holistic process of social transformation from less creative to greater creative participation at the individual and collective levels. Emphasis on the 'creative participation' implies minimization of disorderliness in a social system and maximization of 'creativity' so as to achieve a symbiotic transformation of 'man- nature and society relationship' without generating any anti thesis or conflicts between them. Kashyap, A. (2003).

The focal point of economic development is the economic condition of developing countries regarding economic matters and the development of policies that improve a nation's position economically, socially and institutionally.

Theories of Development were stimulated by the situation in the mid20th century when decolonization occurred and the economic disparity between European and underdeveloped nations became obvious. Others believe that it is more accurate to evaluate development economics as a general provider of organized systems. Todaro, (2000). Consequently, social, economic and political aspects are included in theories of economic development, which apply different models related to different key concepts. Martinussen (1997); Roberts and Hite (2000).

One effective method through which the differentiation between various theories can be recognized is by their classification based on the primary concept of each theory whether internal or external economic development. Several definitions exist for development and offer different focal concepts. For instance, Modernisation Theory stresses the cultural features of each society, such as politics, religion and culture. On the other hand, World Systems Theory and Globalisation seek to evaluate external relationships and to define different points in the development of countries. Consequently, every theory, having identified a driving concept, then proposes specific strategies which should be applied (Olson 1963; Parsons 1964) to achieve economic development. Dependency Theory and World Systems Theory, with an external focus, rely on external reformation policies that deal with relations between dependent and independent countries (Cardoso and Faletto, 1979; Szymanski, 1982). With the understanding of each theory, it becomes pertinent that the dimension of development gradually changed and incorporated many different elements suitable for the better development of human beings through welfare policies.

CHAPTER TWO

Approaches to Tribal Development in India

The Asia Indigenous Peoples Pact (AIPP) states that the largest population of the indigenous people of the world resides in India with eighty million of them scattered across the country closely knit by similar characteristics of socio-political and economic marginalization. The term Scheduled Tribe is used for the purpose of administrating certain specific constitutional privileges, protection and benefits for specific section of peoples, historically considered disadvantaged and backward. "The President notifies the Scheduled Tribes in relation to a particular State or Union Territory and not on an all India basis, by an order, after consultation with the state governments concerned. These orders can be modified subsequently to include or exclude, but only through an act of parliament under Clause 2 of the Article." Bijoy, Gopalakrishnan, Khanna (2010).

In India, the tribal population comprises up of 461 groups (according to the *People of India* project) which constitute 8.0% of the total population of the country, which according to the 2001 census numbered to 83,580,634 members. The central belt of India stretching from Rajasthan and Gujarat in the west to Tripura and West Bengal in the east with states like Maharashtra, Madhya Pradesh, Chhattisgarh, Bihar and Jharkhand at the center is a home to 80% of the total tribal population of the country. States like

Sikkim, Meghalaya, Mizoram, and Nagaland homes the rest 20%. The largest tribal population in South India is found in Andhra Pradesh. Post 1990s witnessed family and beneficiary oriented development schemes that were expanded to bring about welfare opportunities for the tribes. Large scale projects such as mining, manufacturing units, industrial outlets were also started off which provided employment to the tribal people to a certain extent. However, it is studied that the value of the extracted resources from the tribal areas completely outweighed the funds that the central government and the state government allotted to the development of the area. "There is a substantial net flow of resources from the underdeveloped tribal periphery to the more developed non tribal urban and lowland agricultural centers of the country." Jones (1978).

Right from the initial Five-Year Plans, measures for tribal welfare were taken up and so does it continue till today. Keeping aside the British approach and policy of isolation where the tribal groups were kept aside because of the problem of administration, the government of independent India has taken up many projects to bring about development among the tribals. Though the first Prime Minister of Independent India, Pt. Jawaharlal Nehru was busy looking into the overall development of India he did not ignore the tribal population as well. He appointed many Commissions and Committees to look into the matter as to how the tribal issues could be solved. Verrier Elwin suggested the Isolationist or the National Park Approach which he later on changed to Integration Approach. Nehru was however not in favour of such extreme policies but instead believed in following the middle path approach.

Post independent India has witnessed the policies and programmes for tribal development based on Nehruvian guidelines. However, even after six decades of planned developmental strategies adopted in India, the results or outcomes have not been satisfactory. Unequal rate of development has taken the upper hand because of which rampant inequality amongst the inter tribal groups is witnessed. There has been the presence of a well off groups within the same tribal community that have been able to take the advantage of the facilities provided by the government of India for the reserved categories, while on the other hand there is the other group which is still far away, untouched by the blessings of modernity. This is accompanied by rampant corruption, unapproachable bureaucratic system, faulty policies, land distribution pattern, priority of the people and their lifestyles and the lack of interest of the policy implementers. This has ultimately led to the development of a relationship of the exploiter and the exploited where it is difficult to locate the true characters.

The contemporary era has witnessed multiple problems ranging from displacement to famine like poverty condition of the scheduled tribes in some parts of the country. It would be wrong to generalize and place the scheduled tribes on the same economic strata because due to the diversities in the socio-cultural patterns, their economic standards too vary from each other. However, one cannot underestimate the poverty level of the scheduled tribes in the country. Going by the Human Poverty Index (HPI) for the scheduled tribes, it has been seen that it is estimated at 47.79 which is higher than other communities and the Human Development Index (HDI) is estimated at 0.270 which is lower than the HDI of

Scheduled Castes and the non-tribals of the land. The major reason behind such deprived conditions of the scheduled tribes happens to be: land alienation at a rapid rate, disposition of life supporting systems because of displacement, general apathy of the bureaucracy, rise in the atrocities on the tribals, increase in the market forces and lack of success in the planned development efforts.

The evaluation of the success and failure of any policy implemented by the government needs a thorough retrospection for filling in the loopholes if any in the due course of action.

2.1 RETROSPECTION OF TRIBAL DEVELOPMENT IN INDIA

The differences that have emerged as a result of the complex historical process can be understood as the hallmark of Indian socio-political complexities. The phenomenon of tribe and caste has been described by some anthropologist as a construction of the colonial rule because they believe that the characteristics of such groups were defined by the colonial masters through the process of enumeration and classification. This is because the modern idea of separate identity was brought into being by the colonial rule which was later on considered by the leaders of the free nation. 'The colonial administrators used the term tribe to describe people who were heterogeneous in physical and linguistic trades, demographic size, ecological conditions of living, regions inhabited, stages of socio-formation, and levels of acculturation and development.' Bara (2002). The establishment of the Asiatic Society of Bengal (1784) marks a historical event because it was here that for the first time the study group described as tribal studies came into existence. This was followed by notable contributions of eminent scholars like Dalton (1872), Risley (1891), Russel (1916), Thurston (1909) etc. thereby earning the title of the formative period as propounded by Vidyarthi. The phase from 1784 to 1919 was regarded as the *formative period*, from 1920 to 1949 as the *constructive period* and from 1950 onwards as the *analytical period* by Vidyarthi (1982).

The first census report of 1921 described these groups of people as hill and forest tribes while Hutton, the Census Commissioner of 1931 referred to them as primitive tribes with geographical isolation and primitive living conditions as the major criteria of distinction between the tribes and non-tribes. However, the tribal welfare committee of 1951 believed that a clear set of ideas could not be arrived as for categorizing a person into the tribal category. "Tribes in India are thus defined not so much in terms of coherent and well defined criteria but in terms of the administrative classification that divides the population into tribal and non-tribal. Tribes are treated as those groups enumerated in the Indian Constitution in the list of the scheduled tribes. Indeed, the constitution defines a scheduled tribe as such tribe or tribal community or part of or groups within such tribes or tribal communities as deemed under Article 342 to be scheduled tribes." Xaxa (2008). Using the term tribe has generated a lot of dissatisfaction among the scholars, social workers and administrators who have provided alternative terms such as aborigines/ aboriginals (Risley, 1903), backward Hindus (Ghurye, 1963), ethnic minorities (Pathy, 1988), the fourth world (Sengupta, 1982) and tribes in transition (Desai, 1960).

The unique nature, language, culture and identity of the 8.06% of the Indian population that comprises up of the scheduled tribe communities of the land demand a serious understanding and re-examination about their developmental dimension. Developmental strategies have been dedicated to this particular section of society right from the era of independence till date, yet such policies have not been a complete remedy to address the problems faced by these groups of people. Many anthropologists used the term tribal society to refer to societies organized largely on the basis of kinship, especially corporate descent groups. Some political economic theorists hold the view that tribes represent a stage in social evolution intermediate between bands and states. Other theorists such as *Morton Fried*, argue that tribes developed after states, and must be understood in terms of their relationship to them. Tribe is a contested term due to its roots in colonialism. In the popular imagination, tribes reflect a way of life that predates, and is more natural than in modern states. Tribes also reflect primordial social ties, and are clearly bounded, heterogeneous, parochial and stable in nature. In simple words tribe can be defined as a social division in a traditional society consisting of families or communities linked by social, economic, religious or blood ties; or a unit of socio-political organization consisting of a number of families, clans or other groups who share a common ancestry and culture and among whom leadership is typically neither formalized nor permanent.

The Oxford Dictionary defines a tribe as "A group of people in a primitive or barbarous stage of development acknowledging the authority of a chief and usually regarding them as having a common ancestry." D. N. Majumdar (1937) opines the tribes to be a social group with territorial affiliation, endogamous with no specialization of functions ruled by tribal officers hereditary or otherwise, united in language or castes. According to Ralph Linton (1933), Tribe is a group of bands occupying a contiguous territory or territories and having a feeling of unity deriving from numerous similarities in a culture, frequent contacts and a certain community of interests.

Right from the evolutionary stage of social formation in India the tribes were present who still continue to follow different modes of economy like the palaeolithic hunters and gatherers of forest produce to industrial workers. The census data shows that the spatial distribution of the tribes is characterized by a striking tendency of clustering and concentration in pockets that have suffered from isolation historically and are situated in areas where the environment setting is by and large unsuited to sedentary agriculture. Probably this pattern of clustering and concentration has contributed significantly to the lack of adequate interaction between the tribal and non tribal communities within the population of India.

The Government of India has been taking up different policies and programmes for the upliftment and overall development of the tribal population based on the approaches to tribal development. Right from the initial Five-Year Plans, measures for tribal welfare were taken up and so does it continue till today. It would be wrong to blame the government alone as an agency that has not taken sufficient measures to curb the problems faced by the tribals in their day to day lives. Keeping aside the British approach and policy of isolation where the tribal groups were left untouched because of the problem of administration, the government of independent India has taken up many projects to bring about development among the tribals. Though the First Prime Minister of Independent India, Pt. Jawaharlal Nehru appointed many Commissions and

Committees to look into the matter as to how the tribal issues could be solved. Verrier Elwin suggested the Isolationist or the National Park Approach which he later on changed to Integration Approach. Nehru was however not in favour of such extreme policies but instead believed in following the middle path approach.

Post independent India has witnessed the policies and programmes for tribal development based on Nehruvian guidelines. However, even after six decades of planned developmental strategies adopted in India the results or outcomes have not been satisfactory. Unequal rate of development has taken the upper hand because of which rampant inequality amongst the inter-tribal groups is witnessed thereby catalysing the evolution of haves and have-nots within the same tribal group. There has been the presence of a well off group within the same tribal group who have been able to take the advantage of the facilities provided by the government of India for the reserved categories whereas there is the other group that is still far away, untouched by the blessings of modernity, living a life that of the ancient cave ages. This is accompanied by rampant corruption, unapproachable bureaucratic system, faulty policies, land pattern, priority of the people and their lifestyles and the lack of interest of the policy implementers. This has ultimately led to the development of a relationship of the exploiter and the exploited be it within the group or outside. Questions like is it the failure of the government to successfully implement their planned policies or are the elite sections among the tribal groups themselves to be considered the hindrance behind the overall egalitarian development of the tribes. In case of the vacuum created what would be the role of the agencies of development like the civil society and the non-governmental organizations the answers to which has been attempted to be addressed in the book.

Due to the lack of success on the part of the government in bringing about the desired output in the field of tribal development in India i.e. "to translate the constitutional provision into reality" John K. Thomas, (2005), the new trend that was witnessed was the grand scale emergence of the non-governmental organizations in the Indian soil with the primary purpose of reaching out to those sectors where the government had failed to achieve the desired target of development goals. Having analysed the theoretical approaches to Tribal Development and the practical ground reality it is quite evident that there does prevail a huge gap between the two because of which the centre stage of attention has been taken away by the non-governmental organizations in addressing the core questions of tribal development.

The second quarter of the present century to the late seventies portrays an important pattern of tribal development that was adopted by both the official as well as the non-official agencies reflecting upon the existence of genuine weaknesses in different form and at different levels. The adoption of new patterns was considered to be necessary and this necessity changed its features with time. The ideology of various agencies was put to test by time and often regarded to be faulty. Those voluntary organizations that preferred to work in complete isolation from the government in the process of tribal development were criticized but no concrete remedial measure was provided to address the situation. Monetary investments have been made at a speedy rate to bring about the desired development of the scheduled tribes failed in addressing the genuine needs of the beneficiaries. The question of who is to be put to question – is it the State, is it the non-governmental organizations or is it the beneficiary scheduled tribes themselves, provides us with an interesting challenge to be addressed in the book.

The problem of tribal development can be classified into two broad categories: the one that the tribals face, and the other that the functionaries working in for the tribal societies face. Both these categories occupy a place of significance because without addressing the two, the conclusion drawn would be at fault.

It cannot be denied that social development is the primary duty of the state, however in the developing countries marked by the limitation of state and expansion of the NGO sectors, efficiency is expected more from the later. The state is believed to create an environment for development while the NGOs are entrusted to implement the development agenda of the government amongst the grassroots in an economic and efficient manner. At times, the non-governmental organizations are also seen working in close collaboration with the state mechanism as partners in achieving the target of development.

The development of the scheduled tribes cannot be visualized without an active support and an efficient role of the non-governmental organizations in close collaboration with the sincere efforts of the government. This is because one of the prominent reasons behind the underdevelopment of the scheduled tribes happens to be their isolated geographical habitation characterized by hills, forests, river beds and untraceable geographical locations. The case studies conducted proves the fact that the government officials hesitate to settle down in those areas and work for the development of the needy scheduled tribe communities. They demand for immediate transfers and some even go to the extent of resigning from their prestigious post and thereby leaving the office empty. Interestingly, the Indian Prime Minister expresses his awareness about this issue in his lecture in the seminar conducted at the parliament he makes it an attempt to remove the misconception of punishment postings and translates it as an opportunity to serve the fellow countrymen. (*We for Development*, 2018).

In such a situation, the role of the non-governmental organizations stands to be crucial in addressing the immediate needs of the tribal population. The survey conducted provides us with the fact that the scheduled tribe communities largely believe that the non-governmental organizations can perform their duties in a much better manner only if they are genuinely serious about their jobs. This puts a question mark to the integrity of the non-governmental organizations working in the area of tribal development. Those tribal areas that have honest non-governmental organizations working in the area have definitely shown a better quality of life as compared to those where the non-governmental organizations exist only for formality. Moreover, the attitude and approach of the non-governmental organizations towards the beneficiary scheduled tribes generally plays an important role in their overall development because grassroot friendly approach happens to be the need of the hour which needs to be clearly understood by the non-governmental organizations.

2.2 APPROACHES TO TRIBAL DEVELOPMENT IN INDIA: A BRIEF HISTORY

The policies outlined by the changing governments and the welfare oriented state draws heavily upon the philosophies of some of the major developmental approaches of the past. As a matter of fact, the guidelines to tribal development are seen to be in the pillars of the Panchasheel (Panchsheel is an idea developed by Verrier Elwin and propagated by Nehru on tribal development) which is still assumed to have a strong hold upon the policies of the contemporary era. Although historically these approaches may have satisfied the need of the then time frame but to stick to the outdated models would be inappropriate taking into consideration the change-based needs of the contemporary era. The major loopholes witnessed that needs addressal can be stated as follows:

a) **Firstly**, as has been discussed in earlier, development can never be considered to be a static factor. It is always change oriented, and the change has to satisfy the subjects about the problems dependent on time frames and factors. Keeping this logic in mind one fails to understand as to how can the guidelines and approaches to the policies framed in the initial years of independence guided by the approaches of that era be expected to fulfill the problems of the tribes of the twenty first century where the entire scenario has changed. Therefore, in order to get a quality developmental result one must also be ready to give a serious, change oriented, time tested policies of development guided by self reliant approaches to tribal development.

b) **Secondly**, it has been observed that the model of development as has been implemented upon the tribes for tribal development is an externally framed and implemented model by those people majority of whom are non tribals. Therefore, how can they be expected to understand the need of the hour of the subject concerned without living a life in tribal terms and conditions? These externally designed policies formulated by the non tribals in a pyramidical structure with a top-down *approach* have proved to be of little help. Without participatory development, the idea of development itself stands to be incomplete and hence challenged.

c) **Thirdly**, the desperate attempt to wrap the tribal lifestyle in the mainstream model without addressing their basic needs has proved to be a blunder in itself. As a matter of fact, the meaning of development to the tribes may be completely different as that conceived by the mainstream protagonist. However, instead of respecting their culturally oriented developmental ideas, the forceful method of 'made to think in a particular manner as perceived by the mainstream' has made them even more confused, ill equipped, frustrated and backward.

Therefore, a fresh alternative approach is definitely required to address the grassroot problems of the tribes of India which would be for the tribals as perceived best by the tribals with a change in the pyramidical structure of power relations and definitely under the free sky where they can exercise their freedom to think about those issues which are best suited for themselves in preserving their heterogeneous uniqueness, without the un necessary interference and domination of the mainstream forces.

Let us enumerate the major approaches to tribal development-

2.2.1 POLITICAL APPROACH

The Political Approach to Tribal Development must be understood against the backdrop of Pre and Post independence era of India. The colonial masters through their creation of "excluded and partially excluded" areas intended to give separate political representation to the tribes and in a way (as pointed out by the nationalists) created a difference between the tribals and the non tribals on the one hand and between the tribals themselves on the other. After independence the Constitution of India provided for the tribals a number of constitutional safeguards for the protection and development of this category of people who were historically backward and were unrepresented in the governmental arena.

2.2.2 ADMINISTRATIVE APPROACH

Alongside the political approach the administrative approach also had a major impact on the tribal development of India. The essence of this approach relies on the understanding of the political leadership about the strategies to promote development among the tribals, the implementation of the various schemes of development by the government and the role of the administrative mechanism in the successful implementation of the developmental policies. At the state level the governor has been entrusted with the responsibility of ensuring development in the areas inhabited by the tribal population to be administered under the Fifth and Sixth Schedule of the constitution. Apart from this, the Governor ensures that the Chief Minister makes special scheme for tribal areas. There is also a tribal welfare ministry operating at the state and central levels to take care of the tribal development.

2.2.3 RELIGIOUS APPROACH

This approach has been attended by different religious agencies like the Christian Missionaries, Arya Samaj, Ramkrishna Mission and other local religious institutions that are engaged in the welfare of the tribals. They engage in both spiritual and material types of work and carry out welfare activities. However, a critical review of this approach has proved the fact that the development brought about in the remote tribal areas is done by the various religious fronts at the cost of converting the faith of the subject from animism to the mainstream religious dogmas as propagated by the latter. Though in its face value it may not seem to be much of a problem but if observed carefully then this shall have an alarming negative impact upon the cultural dynamics of the tribals which in turn would mean a faulty mode of development eradicating the cultural uniqueness of the heterogeneous tribal communities of the country.

2.2.4 VOLUNTARY AGENCIES APPROACH

Under this approach, the social workers, social welfare agencies like NGO's, Social Movement agencies etc. work in the tribal areas for the upliftment of the weaker sections of the society. They offer services like capacity building, skill development, community development, awareness programmes and other humanitarian activities`.

2.2.5 ANTHROPOLOGICAL APPROACH

In as early as 1807, the significance of the anthropological studies was recognized when a formal declaration which when put in lines stated that, "such knowledge would be of great use in the future administration in the country", was made by the court of directors of the East India Company. As a result, Dr. Francis Buchanon was appointed by the Governor General–in Council to undertake an ethnographic survey "to inquire into the condition of the inhabitants of Bengal and their religion." Since then, many prominent anthropology oriented administrators such as Resley, Thurston, Dalton, Grigson, Gurdon and many more on deputation prepared handbooks, gazetteers, monographs etc. on the Indian tribes and castes. It must be noted here that due to the pioneering efforts of the anthropology oriented administrators and later on the anthropologists that wholesome knowledge could be gathered on and later developed by the researchers of the later period.

However, the Anthropological approach is not free from criticisms about its contribution to the tribal studies. This approach has been condemned at the administrative level specially the one cited out by Verrier Elwin about the isolation of tribes for development. However, post 1949, some major papers were written down by the anthropologists on the measures of tribal welfare policies and programmes.

2.2.6 ISOLATION- ASSIMILATION APPROACH: ELWIN GHURYE DEBATE

The formulation and implementation of policies became very much crucial for the tribes in the post independence era. However, the much awaited debate on the inclusion and exclusion of tribal people from the mainstream development took place even prior to independence resting largely on the shoulders of two eminent personalities namely G.S. Ghurye and Verrier Elwin. The mighty debate traces its origin in the work of Elwin *The Baiga*, published in 1939 which was circulated in a pamphlet named *The Aboriginals* (1944). In this book, Elwin made some suggestions regarding the kind of approach to be adopted for the development of the tribes of India. The focus of attention was on the primary issue as to whether the then present condition of the tribes living in isolation would and should be continued in the post independent era or whether they should be put in the larger mainstream for development and thereby be able to enjoy the facilities as enjoyed by the mainstream population. Elwins approach was known by the names *Leave them Alone Approach, National Park Approach, or Isolationist Approach* which in literal term meant letting the tribes live on their own not infringing upon their economic space and allowing them to grow on their self-created, self-designed developmental paradigms.

After having studied the Baiga tribe, the concept of isolation struck Elwins mind. The two major factors that immensely influenced Elwin in building up this approach were

- ❖ The offensive attitude of the British Rulers who wanted the tribes to be left alone because trying to administer the borders and remote area would not be of much benefit to them.
- ❖ The second was the attitude of the then active anthropologists who preferred to keep the tribals as a separate sample universe for their study.

Elwin was charged with advocating the policy of isolation. However, Elwin defended himself on the lines that his suggestions were based in desperation as 'the Baigas had very little left of their own when the book was written in 1939.' It was important to keep them alive first free from exploitation and oppression and then talk about preserving their culture later on. However, this also marked a shift in the position of Elwin and no more did he advocate about complete isolation. It is to be pointed out that Elwin perceives about two types of tribes- the majority tribes and the minority tribes. A careful study of his work points out the fact that the policy of isolation was meant only for the minority tribes 'a small section of the tribal population.' For the majority of the tribal population, the policy advocated by Elwin was no different from the policies outlined for the general population, as he believed that the problems faced by the tribal population could not be considered to be different from those faced by the general village population. 'What Elwin suggested was not the same policy for the entire tribal population of the country.' Elwin, (1960).

Against this background, G.S. Ghurye clearly advocated the policy of assimilation. Ghurye considered the tribes to be Hindus and precisely backward Hindus. The major reason for becoming backward Hindus was because of the fact that the tribes mostly settled down in the interiors, hill sides and remote forests making them completely cut off from the rest of the mainland Indian population. He advocated that the tribes should be assimilated in the larger society so that their living conditions would develop from a completely hopeless situation of abject poverty towards betterment. In his opinion Ghurye placed the tribes at the lowest position on the tribe-caste-class continuum which is a conceptual paradigm that is used for understanding the process of change in tribal life. This meant a movement of the tribals to modernity from tradition and to a higher form of religion from pantheism and to an ethically and morally superior class from that of a crude lifestyle. This phase can be regarded to be the *assimilation –integration stage* of the tribal population in the national mainstream.

These major approaches have been interpreted and reinterpreted by eminent scholars in the understanding of tribal development in India.

D.N. Majumdar (1944) has studied the efforts towards tribal development under the following two heads- 1. Reform Approach and 2. Administrative Approach.

S.C. Dubey (1960) has listed out four major approaches namely- 1. The Social Service Approach 2. The Political Approach 3. The Religious Approach 4. The Anthropological Approach

L.P. Vidyarthi (1982) has used the help of four major approaches in addressing tribal welfare. These are as follows- 1. Anthropologists Approach 2. Social Workers Approach 3. Missionaries Approach 4. Administrative Machinery for Tribal Welfare.

It can be pointed out that the understanding of the approaches to tribal development by the eminent scholars somewhere or the other traces its roots and also bears similarity to the above mentioned major approaches. Let us now look into the post independent era and the strategies of development as adopted by the independent state of India.

2.2.7 STATE'S APPROACH TO TRIBAL DEVELOPMENT IN THE POST INDEPENDENCE ERA

The government of independent India under the leadership of Jawaharlal Nehru did not consider either of the two policies as perceived by Elwin and Ghurye to be adequate to address the issue of tribal development especially in the post independent era. The constitutional provisions for the tribes mark a point in support of this stand of the state. When we look into the approach formulated by Nehru for the tribals, one can see that Nehru avoided the two extreme courses of either total isolation or total integration in the mainstream developmental process. Pt. Jawaharlal Nehru spelled out the policy as follows: "We cannot allow matters to drift in the tribal areas or lest not take interest in them. At the same time, we should avoid over administering the areas and in particular sending too many outsiders into the territory. It is between the two extreme positions we shall have to function". He believed that the tribes should not be kept as mere anthropological specimens for the purpose of intellectual observation but should be protected from external exploitation adhered to by the outside world (referring to the non tribals). Nehru believed in gradual change thereby providing selective and voluntary introduction of advanced technology for development. In other words, Nehru's development policy for the tribals was based on gradualism and light interference by the state. The main focus of attention of the then government was to search for a solution as to how to bring the blessings and advantages of modern medicines agriculture and education to the tribes, without destroying the rare and precious values of tribal life. The constitutional provisions included 'statutory recognition, proportional representation in the legislatures, the right to use their own language for education and other purposes, the right to profess their own faith and the right to pursue development in accordance to their own genius. The Constitution also empowered the state to make provisions for reservation in jobs and appointment in favour of tribal communities. The Directive Principle of State Policy of the Constitution required that the educational and economic interest of the weaker sections of society, including tribals be especially promoted (Article 46).' Xaxa, (2008).

A close examination of the provision of the constitution on tribal development points out the fact that the approach of development adopted is much more a policy of integration than isolation or assimilation without using the term integration anywhere in the area concerned. As a matter of fact, no official document is found which elaborates on the idea of integration explicitly. However, unofficially the approach towards tribal development reflected in the policies tilt towards the direction of integration.

The guide to the policies of the state towards tribal development can be found in the five principles mentioned by Nehru in his forward to Elwin's *A Philosophy for NEFA* underlying the constitutional provisions. These **guiding principles** are as follows-

1. People should develop along the lines of their own genius and we should avoid imposing anything on them. We should try to encourage in every way, their own traditional arts and culture.

2. Tribal rights in land forest should be respected.

3. We should try to train and build up a team of their own people to do the work of administration and development. Some technical personnel from outside will no doubt be needed especially in the beginning. But we should avoid introducing too many outsiders in to tribal territory.

4. We should not over administer these areas or overwhelm them with a multiplicity of schemes. We should rather work through and not in rivalry to their own social and cultural institutions, and

5. The results should not be guided by the amount of money spent but instead by the quality of human character that is involved.

Taking these guidelines into consideration the state has formulated policies for tribal development in India which shall be dealt below.

After having clearly understood the different types of conventional approaches to tribal development in India that have been applied in the process of policy formulations for the development of the scheduled tribes over the years, we now put forward some of the alternative approaches that can be put into use in the process of tribal development in order to bring about a positive change in the quality of human development.

2.3 UNDERSTANDING TRIBAL DEVELOPMENT FROM THE TRIBAL PERSPECTIVE

The idea of development as we have studied in our earlier sections is a reflection of the understanding of development from the view point of the government, the academicians, the external agencies and any such organs that have assumed to conceptualize it from above not being a member to its impact. The voices of the marginalized have always been neglected and unheard which has resulted in the creation of a huge gap in the idea of development understood by the external agencies on the one hand, and that which is interpreted by the beneficiaries themselves on the other hand. This is because there has not taken place a required amount of consultation of the beneficiaries taking them into confidence by the policy framers thereby resulting in the mismatched idea of development which fail to address the needs of the scheduled tribes and in turn widen the gap between the two.

The earlier sections of this chapter have been completely dedicated to the interpretation of scholarly understanding of the meaning of development. However, the pertinent question that arises here which needs to be addressed first is development for whom? Probably the answer to this question in this section would be development for the tribals or what we generally perceive it as tribal development. Since the meaning of development has transcended from mere economic growth to social betterment, to the protection of human rights with the help of participation of the beneficiaries, this has clearly revealed the fact that development cannot be successful without the participation of the people who are to be developed. This is because history stands a testament to the fact that top down approach where the entire decision of planning and implementation is taken up by the alien agents of development has failed to understand the immediate requirement of the beneficiaries and focus upon the pre-design unnecessary enforcement of the policy programmes.

This backlash can be evaluated from the alarming rate of failure of the development agencies in bringing about development of the tribal population.

Therefore, it is very important for us to understand the emotions of the tribal population of the country by making the developmental approach a participatory one, whereby the real needs of the beneficiaries would be addressed first.

2.4 TOWARDS AN ALTERNATIVE APPROACH

The existing system based on power relationship with one organ trying to be more powerful than the other needs to be reminded of that power distribution should be on healthy lines with a strong inclusion of the less powerful for the very survival of the power structure. Power here as well has many interrelated dimensions are directly or indirectly linked to each other. As a matter of fact, one dimension of power acts as a variable to the other and the rise in one has a direct impact on the other. In such a situation where power relation guides and directs the other dimensions of development, tribal development also requires to be readdressed from the lenses of power relationship. In doing so, special reference must be made to Prof. Anthony Giddens who worked extensively in the decade of the 1970's and the 1980's vigorously trying to fulfil the loopholes of constraints found evidently in the structural theory ofTalcot Parsons. The Structural Functional theory of Parson talked about the system and the actors inside the system but fail to provide us with the suitable answer as to what would be the role of the individuals that affect the society and in turn create a bench mark in history. To fulfil this unanswered loophole Prof. Giddens suggests his Structuration theory where he uses the term structure and agency respectively. Unlike Parson's Structural Functional analysis, Giddens structure and agency are well connected through cooperation rather than two discreet objects of antagonism. As a matter of fact, Giddens regards the agency and structure to be two faces of the same coin and that the line of distinction between the agency and structure is simply analytical and not distinct in nature. This is regarded to be the duality of structure of Giddens Structuration theory. He compares his idea of structuration as an orchestra where we see the presence of different instruments (agency), producing a single music (structure), yet the variations in the tone of the music produced is distinct and clear representing every instrument. In the structuration process, good and new behaviours that are beneficial to both the agency and the structure are incorporated, while the harmful and useless behaviours are patted out of the system. In his words a system represents the major institutions of the society, the structure denotes a guard that combats perpetuation of society through individual behaviour and structuration means the actors in a close interaction with the system.

2.5 THE STRUCTURATIONIST APPROACH

Transcending the dualism of structure and agency, Giddens (1976, 1979, 1981, 1984) developed his theory basing on the premise. Giddens wanted to develop a hybrid theory capable of reconciling, on the one hand, a focus on the structuring that are the very condition of social and political interaction, with on the other hand, a sensitivity to the intentionality, reflexivity, autonomy and agency of actors. Hay (1995). Giddens observed that in social analysis, the term *structure* referred generally to "rules and resources" and more specifically to "the structuring properties allowing the 'binding' of time-space in social systems". These properties make it possible for similar social practices to exist across time and space and that lend them "systemic" form. (Giddens 1984) Agents—groups or individuals—draw upon these structures to perform social actions through embedded memory, called *memory traces*. Memory traces are thus the vehicle through which social actions are carried out. Structure is also, however, the result of these social practices. Thus, Giddens conceives of the *duality of structure* as being the essential recursive element of social life, as constituted in social practices: structure is both medium and outcome of reproduction of practices. Structure enters simultaneously into the constitution of the agent and social practices, and 'exists' in the generating moments of this constitution. (Giddens 1979). Giddens uses "the duality of structure" to emphasize structure's nature as both medium and outcome. Structures exist both internally within agents as memory traces that are the product of phenomenological and hermeneutic inheritance (Stones 2005) and externally as the manifestation of social actions. Similarly, social structures contain agents and/or are the product of past actions of agents. Giddens holds this duality, alongside "structure" and "system," as the core of structuration theory. (Giddens 1984) Structure and Agency are according to Giddens mentally related or ontologically intertwined. They comprise a duality. The keys to Giddens idea are the twin concepts – structuration and the duality of structure. In The Constitution of Society (1984) Giddens defines the duality of structure in the following way- structure as the medium and outcome of the conduct it recursively organizes. The structural properties of social system do not exist outside of action but are chronically implicated in its production and reproduction. (1984-374). The structuration on the other hand was defined as "the structuring of social relations across time and space, in virtue of the duality of structure". Giddens chooses to highlight the duality of structure and claims that "social structures are both constituted by human agency, and yet at the same time are the very medium of its constitution." (1967) what Giddens seems to suggest is that structure and agency may indeed be ontologically intertwined.

His theory has been adopted not only by those with structuralist inclinations but also by those who wish to situate such structures in human practice rather than to reify them as an ideal type or material property. (This is different, for example, from actor–network theory which appears to grant certain autonomy to technical artifacts). Social systems have patterns of social relation that change over time; the changing nature of space and time determines the interaction of social relations and therefore structure. Hitherto, social structures or models were either taken to be beyond the realm of human control—the positivistic approach—or posit that action creates them—the interpretivist approach. The duality of structure emphasizes that there are different sides to the same central question of how social order is created. Gregor Mc. Lennan (1997) suggested renaming this process "the duality of structure *and agency*", since both aspects are involved in using and producing social actions. (Mc. Lennan 1997.) Giddens seems to suggest that while Structure and Agency may indeed be ontologically intertwined, but it is difficult to capture the real duality of Structure and Agency as we can only view either from the perspective of Agency or the perspective of the Structure at one particular time. We may change our viewpoints to capture the other side but we cannot view both the sides at the same point. The best we can hope to recognize is a dialectical relationship between Structure and Agency which of course Giddens does not recognize. There seems to be a kind of methodological bracketing which leads to the paradoxical effect of enforcing an artificial separation between life world and system elements Derek Layder (1998).

Taking a clue from this understanding of the interrelationship between Agency and Structure, one can approach the issue of Tribal development from this perspective. The discourse on tribal development and the programmes on tribal development need to be analysed keeping in mind that the tribal people are embedded within their contexts, and giving too much emphasis to the context would rob off the tribal people of their free will to challenge the existing order and devise a new path of development for them. At the same time, it also needs to be understood that both the Agency and the Structure that is the tribal people and their contexts are intertwined and one seems to influence the other and vice versa.

Tribal development in India with its more than seven hundred and fifty different communities can be equated to the agency while the government and the non-governmental organizations represent the system where the government acts as a structure that guards the system from disturbances. Structuration here denotes a cooperative relationship between the agency (the scheduled tribes) and the structure (the State). The role of the non-governmental organizations can be incorporated in the system. Therefore, this alternative approach to tribal development provides us with an idea on the guidelines of Prof. Giddens where there must exist a friendly relationship between the tribals, the State including the non-governmental organizations.

The uniqueness of the tribal communities must be preserved like the sound of individual instrument producing sweet symphony. They must be granted the right to choose the best for themselves along the lines of Right to Development as a human right. Having said this, the role of the non-governmental organizations cannot be underestimated because it forms an integral part of the system designed to bring about development if the agency.

CHAPTER THREE

State and Tribal Development in India

The chief agency of development of any area of the nation is the state and the measures that it undertakes for the upliftment of the subject in question. The detailed study of tribal development cannot be made without taking into consideration the role of the state through its policies, plans and implementation over the years. This must be followed by genuine review of the implemented policies and the study of its success and failure accordingly.

3.1 TRACING THE ROLE OF THE STATE IN THE GENESIS OF TRIBAL STUDIES

The Scheduled Tribes inhabit about 15-20% of the land area of the Indian sub- continent. The Census 2011 testifies the existence of 10.4 crore of scheduled tribe population out of which 5.2 crore are male and 5.18 crore are females in these heterogeneous communities of the nation making it a total of 8.6% of the total population of the country. 89.7% of the scheduled tribe communities live in the rural zones while only 0.03% of them are found in the urban areas. Technically, addressing the India tribes as the indigenous population would prove to be incorrect. The Government of India does not consider any specific section of its population as 'indigenous people' as that generally understood and implied in its usage in the United

Nations Organization. Operationally, however, those sections of the people are considered to represent the indigenous group who fall within the administrative category of 'Scheduled Tribes'. Therefore, in the Indian context the scheduled tribes are accepted to represent the indigenous group operationally.

The working definition provided by the Martinez Cobo (2011) study under the United Nations defines the Indigenous communities, peoples and nations as "those which, having a historical continuity with pre-invasion and pre-colonial societies that developed on their territories, consider themselves distinct from other sectors of the societies now prevailing on those territories, or parts of them. They form at present non-dominant sectors of society and are determined to preserve, develop and transmit to future generations their ancestral territories, and their ethnic identity, as the basis of their continued existence as peoples, in accordance with their own cultural patterns, social institutions and legal system." It has been noticed that although the indigenous people have been given their due recognition as people identified with a unique culture, dialect, religion and positive heterogeneous uniqueness in them, yet a practical view points out the fact that historically they have suffered exploitation, violation of human rights and humiliation in all forms. The indigenous people all over the world represent the most vulnerable and disadvantaged group of people. The international community has now taken up the responsibility to recognize and address the special measures to protect and preserve the rights and cultures of the indigenous people all over the world with a positive group effort from individual countries.

India, a member of the United Nations Organization leaves no stone unturned in bringing the operationally indigenous people and technically scheduled tribe people at par with the mainstream development, carefully retaining their cultural uniqueness.

The discourses on the origin of tribal studies are varied and multiple, each one with a definite perspective of its own. Some mainstream protagonists speak volumes on the single sided positive dynamics of the state initiatives on tribal development while on the other hand reality speaks the opposite at the ground level. It would be wrong on the part of a researcher to justify a lopsided claim of any organization on its success of any mission.

Prof. Virginius Xaxa (2008). elaborated his ideas on the genesis of tribal development in his book *State, Society and Tribes: issues in Post Colonial India* (2008) making an in depth study on tribal development, in explaining the genesis of tribal development as a subject on its own. The phenomena of caste and tribe as a colonial construction have been advocated by some of the early anthropologists. They are of the view that the British solidified the concept of caste and tribes through the process of their colonial classification and enumeration. Beteille (1986) is of the view that this idea stands to be truer in the case of the tribes than the castes because a good number of complex and sophisticated literature on castes were already present even before the advent of the British rule in India. As a matter of fact, it was the colonial state that initiated the separate and distinct identity of the tribes which was later on carried by the successive governments of independent India. The colonial administrators used the term tribe to describe people who were 'heterogeneous in physical and linguistic traits, demographic size, ecological conditions, stages of social formation, and level of acculturation and development.'

The tribal studies can be fragmented into three phases namely:

- The Formative Phase (1784-1919),
- The Constructive Phase (1920-1949) and
- The Analytical Phase (1950 onwards). Xaxa, (2008)

The establishment of the Asiatic Society of Bengal 1784 marked a historic landmark in the study of groups in a formal manner, which later on came to be described as tribal studies. A plethora of serious studies were conducted mostly in the form of monographs and handbooks. Some of the noteworthy works can be stated to be as follows: *Descriptive Ethnology of Bengal* (Dalton, 1872), *Tribes and Castes of Bengal* (Risley, 1891), *Tribes and Castes of the Central Province of India* (Russel and Hira La, 1916), *Castes and Tribes of Southern India* (Thurston, 1909).

The early eighteenth century writings of the British in India did not distinguish between the castes and the tribes. The two terms were in fact used synonymously. The differences were known much later when it was seriously identified that the tribes bared traits that were significantly distinct from the mainstream Indian population. This was realized only after the result of the first ever census conducted in the Indian soil. Post 1901, a clearer description was provided for categorizing a group as a tribal group. 'The tribes were identified and described as those groups that practiced animism; later the phrase tribal religion was used in its place.' The 1921 census described this group as hill and forest tribes, and in 1931 when Hutton was the census commissioner, tribes were also referred to as primitive tribes.

Furthermore, the other important elements such as the primitive living conditions and geographical isolations were added to the categories of compartmentalization. Religion was considered to be the most important element of differentiating a tribe from a non tribe. They practiced a faith in nature worship completely different from Hinduism, Islam and Christianity. 'If a group were shown to be Hindu in its beliefs and religious practices, it was identified as a caste. If it were shown to be animist, it was treated as a tribe.' The inclusion of the scheduled tribes in the Indian constitution traces its origin to the administrative and political considerations. The Constitution defines a scheduled tribe 'as such tribe or tribal community or part of or groups within such tribes or tribal communities as are deemed under Article 342 to be Scheduled Tribes'. Till date there has not been the formulation of a standard definition of tribes because each school of thought is in ideological confrontation with the other as regards the distinctive features to be prescribed as a parameter to be qualified by a group to earn the title of a Scheduled Tribe keeping in mind the changing global phenomena. The state does not define in a coherent manner the meaning of tribes and does not provide clear cut criteria for a group to be termed as a tribe. It has been observed that only for the sake of administrative purpose has the state distinguished people as tribes and non tribes.

3.2 DEFINING STATE AND GOVERNMENT

For the holistic development of any area, proper planning and policy formulation happens to be the crux of the subject. Tribal development does not stand to be an exception in this regard. Since the pre-independence era itself, special policies were devised for the secluded regions inhabited by the tribal population. The post-independence era witnessed the tribal developmental policies formulated on the guidelines of the Nehruvian approach of neither complete isolation nor complete acculturation of these communities with the mainland settlement of the Indian population. It is to be noted that after the interval of every Five Year Plan period, special budget allocations and developmental policies have been formulated by the government to bring about the development of the scheduled tribe communities of the nation. The plan period has changed hands to the NITI Aayog but the focus of attention still happens to be the upliftment of these marginalized sections of the people on a better footing. At this juncture, it becomes very important to review the policies of the government for the development of the scheduled tribe communities for a better understanding of the impact of the policies formulated for their development. This dimension of reviewing the policies of the government for the development of the tribal population opens up a new avenue of research that can be taken up separately.

Some of the noteworthy policies that trace its origin in the initial five year plans shall also be discussed in here. However, before starting off with the critical analysis of the policies of the state with regard to tribal development, one must draw a conceptual clarity as to what do we really understand by the term state and whether it is all correct to use the term government and state interchangeably. In other words, a clear differentiation between the state and the government is very much pertinent in the understanding of the policies for the development of the tribes. Under this background, let us first try to understand the meaning of the state.

From a general understanding, the meaning of the state is understood by the function that it performs. The purview of the state is witnessed to embrace almost each and every activity of human life be it education, economic activities, sanitation, welfare, defence etc. As a matter of fact, the term state has been used to refer to a wide range of interpretations like- a collection of institutions, a philosophical idea, a territorial unit, an instrument of coercion or oppression etc. Max Stirner (1845) has taken a step ahead and described the state on the basis of its functioning- "The purpose of the state is always the same: to limit the individual, to tame him, to subordinate him, to subjugate him." (Max Stirner defined the state in his book *The Ego and His Own. (1845)*). The reason behind the multi-dimensional understanding of the state is because of the fact that the state has been understood in three different perspectives namely the *idealist, functionalist and organizational.*

The main profounder of the idealist approach is GWF Hegel who identified and advocated about the three moments of social existence: family (particular altruism), civil society (universal egoism) and the state (universal altruism). The idealist approach is criticized for its uncritical reverence towards the state. The functionalist perspective focuses on the role/ purpose/ function of the states' existence. The maintenance of social order is regarded to be the most pertinent function of the state institution. The state from this approach is regarded as a set of institutions that uphold order and maintain stability in the society. This approach is however criticized on the ground that it fails to gather clarity as to which institution should be included under the purview of the state and which ones to be excluded. The organizational perspective defines the state in its broadest sense as the apparatus of the government. It indicates a set of institutions that are funded on public expenses and are responsible for the 'collective organization of social existence.' This approach is successful enough in clearly demarcating the major line of difference between the state and the civil society. (The modern notion of sovereign statehood was formalized in the Treaty of Westphalia 1648.)

After having understood the three major approaches of the understanding of the state the next important question that needs to be specifically addressed here is that can we use the term state and government interchangeably to refer to the policies of development formulated by such superior organization or institution for welfare activities? In other words, would it be technically correct to refer to the state as the government and vice versa? Reference must be made to Heywood, (2007) who distinguishes between the two terms with the idea of constitutional government. To him, the distinction between state and government is not just confined to the academic globe but instead is deep seated in the heart of the idea of constitutional government. (The power structure of the government can be checked only when it is debarred of encroaching upon the authority of the state which is unlimited and absolute). Some of the major lines of differences between the state and the government stand to be as follows-

a) The state is more extensive than the government because it encompasses within its association the entire institutions of the public realm. Government on the other hand is a part of the state.

b) The state is a permanent and an ever-continuing entity while the government is a temporary body which is likely to be reformed and remodeled with a change in the political scenario.

c) The authority of the state is put into operation with the help of the government. The perpetuation of the states' existence in the form of the formulation and the implementation of the state policies are the brain child of the government.

d) The permanent interests of the society like the common good and the general will are represented by the state. On the other hand, the government represents the partisan interest of those in power.

Examining the policies of the state towards tribal development we come across a clear fact that the guidelines on the basis of which developmental policies were/are formulated and implemented remains more or less intact right from the initial years of independence i.e. the state run and represented by the Nehru government. With the passage of time, political hands changed from different political elites and so did the five year plans also succumb to changes. With this, the tribal welfare policies also widened but cannot be regarded to have changed completely as the approaches and the guidelines have remained the same. This has also created a major hindrance because the genuine and immediate needs of the tribals have not been attended to due to the top down policy of the state or the changing governments. The static policies seem to have done minimum for the upliftment of the marginalized people. If only with the changing of the government the policies and approaches would be changed trying to address the immediate needs of the subject then this would have brought about a meaningful change in the lives of the tribes of India. For addressing this problem, a serious critical analysis is required alongside the positive and dedicated approach of change in the attitude of the government. Having understood the major line of differences between the two mighty terms state and the government, carrying its individuality, therefore, the term state and government would be used as in accordance with the requirement of the flow of the debate.

3.3 CONSTITUTIONAL PROVISIONS FOR THE SCHEDULED TRIBES

Scheduled Tribe is generally used as an administrative term for administering certain specific constitutional benefits, protection and privileges for the wellbeing of a particular section of population those of which that are historically considered to be backward and the most disadvantaged group. Article 366 (25) of the Indian Constitution defines the Scheduled Tribes as "such tribes or tribal communities or parts of, a group within such tribes, or tribal communities as are deemed under Article 342 to be Scheduled Tribes for the purpose of this constitution". (Khanna, 2010). The status of Scheduled Tribe is conferred to a person on the basis of his birth in a Scheduled Tribe community, and the inclusion of this community under the Scheduled Tribe category must be declared as such by the President of India through a public notification. It is the President who notifies the Scheduled Tribes in relation to a particular state/ Union Territory, and not on all India basis, by an order after consultation with the State Governments concerned. (Gopalakrishnan, 2010).

With regard to the term indigenous people the government of India officially does not provide any specific section of its population this title as she firmly believes that all its native population are in some way or the other indigenous. However, technically to smoothen the administrative operation in dissecting a particular section as indigenous a special category of the Scheduled Tribes is considered to be indigenous people, the indigenousness of which is recognized as something different and distinct from regionalism. However, it must be pointed out that not all indigenous people are recognized as the Scheduled Tribes and vice-versa, the homogenization under an umbrella socio-cultural categorization being a serious mistake.

The constitution has conferred upon the tribes of India the fundamental rights clearly recognizing them to be at power with the other mainstream members thereby giving cognizance to the idea of equality which is very much essential for an inclusive society. Furthermore, the constitution contains many provisions specially prescribed for the tribal people. These include- 'provisions for their statutory recognition (Article 342), for their proportional representation in the Parliament and the state legislatures (Article 330 & 332), restrictions on the right of the ordinary citizens to move and settle in tribal areas or to acquire property there (Article 19(5)), the protection of tribal language, dialect and culture (Article 29), and for reservation in general (Article 14(4)) and in jobs and appointments in favour of tribal communities in particular (Article16(4)).' Xaxa, (2008).

The post independence era witnessed a change in hands of the policy of isolation and non interference of the British era replaced by a policy of development through the method of integration. Article 244 happens to be one of the fundamental provisions of the Indian constitution that provides for the scheduled areas in accordance to Schedule V and Schedule VI for the administration of the tribal area. Articles 5, 46, 275,330, 332, 335, 339 and 342 of the Indian constitution provided specific provisions for the advancement of

Scheduled Castes and Scheduled Tribes. Nearly 209 Articles and 2 special schedules of the constitution of India are directly relevant to the Scheduled Tribes some of which are listed under the following heads.

- Social Safeguards: Article 14, 15, 15(4), 16, 16(4), 16(4A), 25 – 28, 29 – 30, 338A, 339(1), 340
- Economic Safeguards: Article 46, 275(1), 335.
- Political Safeguards: Article 330, 332, 243D, 243T, 243M(4) (b), 243ZC (3), 244, 371A, 371B, 371C, 371F, 371G, 371H,
- Fifth Schedule: Provision as to the Administration and Control of Scheduled Areas and STs,
- Sixth Schedule: Provision as to the Administration of Tribal Areas in the States of Assam, Meghalaya, Tripura and Mizoram. Thankur & Moluram, (1997).

3.4 GOVERNMENTAL APPROACH TOWARDS TRIBAL DEVELOPMENT

The policies taken up by the state for the upliftment of the tribal people can be broadly studied under three major heads namely protective safeguards, mobilizational strategies and developmental measures. Xaxa, (2008). Let us elaborate it in the following manner:

- **Protective Safeguards**- With the background that the constitution aims to protect and safeguard the interest of the tribal people, laws have been formulated and implemented to prevent alienation of land from tribes to the non tribes. In some parts of the countries such laws prevailed since the

British era which was furthermore restored in the tribal lands in the post independence era. The special administration of tribal areas referred to as the Fifth and Sixth scheduled areas (Articles 224 and 224(a)) has furthermore provided protective safeguards to the tribal population.

- **Mobilizational Strategies**- In the fields of education, employment and politics, reservations have been provided to the tribal people, which means that a certain percentage of seats are reserved for the scheduled tribes. This policy of reservation is called mobilizational strategies. The reservation of seats in terms of politics i.e. in the parliament and in the state legislatures were actually meant to be in force for a period of ten years which remains renewed at the end of every ten years. 7.5% of seats were reserved for the Scheduled tribes in all spheres which remains the same in spite of the change in the population size.

- **Developmental Measures**- The developmental programmes and policies designed for the upliftment of the tribal people is what is understood by the developmental measures. The developmental policies for the tribes of India taken up by the government can be studied under two broad heads: the first phase being the origin till 1990s and the second phase being that of the post 1990s era.

The introduction of the Community Development Programmes placing the blocks as the main administrative unit can be regarded to be the primary step towards tribal development in India. The Fifth Plan in the year 1974-79 gradually replaced the community development programme with the Tribal Sub Plan (TSP).

The tribal sub plan has proved to be comparatively successful in the channelization of funds proportionate to the tribal population from the general development sector. The state tribal sub plans have also been granted provisions by the central government. The sixth Plan in the years 1980-1985 witnessed the launching of the various poverty alleviation programmes. A major breakthrough was experienced in the Seventh Plan in the years 1986-1990 where the two mighty national institutions were set up. These were the Tribal Cooperative Marketing Development Federation (TRIFED) with the aim of paying remunerative to the tribes for the forest and agricultural products; and the National Scheduled Caste and Scheduled Tribes Finance and Development Cooperation (NSFDC) with the aim of providing credit support for the generation of employment.

In India, tribal development programmes have been merely an extension of the rural development programmes meant for the country as a whole. Goswami, (1990).

The main philosophy of the Government of India, tracing its genesis to Nehru, on the development of the tribal communities has been that of "integration with the mainstream". This clearly reflects the emphasis on the maintenance and the preservation of human values and the multi-cultural milieu of the Indian tribes. Nehru's philosophy on the tribes of India was to preserve the tribal communities throughout the world and integrate them with the nation's mainstream, without in anyway interfering or devaluing the rich cultural heritage. Vasudeva Rao, (2005).

The Constitution of India defines the broad considerations that should guide the efforts and attentions towards Tribal Development. From the First Five Year Plan (1952) till the Seventh Five Year Plan

(1990), sustained specialized attention of the planners have been invested on material and financial resources towards the development of the tribes by reaching out to every family of the tribal community.

In the analysis of the policies of the government on tribal development, it is very important to state the fact that there are two major policies that affect the wellbeing of the tribal communities of India. The tribal development programmes may be divided and studied under two heads namely:

- Programmes directly benefitting the tribes and
- Programnmes indirectly benefitting the tribes.

The former addresses the tribes and tribal areas directly by making an effort to improve the economic condition of the tribes by directly touching on the family of the tribes and the area of living of the tribes. These include policies that primarily help in land redistribution, land reclamation land development and soil conservation measures, supply of agricultural inputs, promotion of village and cottage industries, animal husbandry, business etc.

Talking about the area based programmes to tribal development, focus is primarily upon the construction of tube well, sanitation and roads, minor irrigation and lift irrigation scheme, construction of Sishu Shiksha Kendra for infants and children , Anganwadi centres and primary schools and other community development programmes. The programmes indirectly benefitting the tribes are the ones that are basically general in nature targeting the entire underdeveloped and rural zones of India which are equally important for restoring confidence among the tribes and bringing them in closer contact with the outside world. However, the general programmes of development like the Community Development Programme of 1952, Intensive Agricultural Development Programme(1960-1961), Rural Electrification Corporation (1969), Marginal Farmer and Agriculture Labour Agency(1973-74) were limited to economic development only.

3.5 POLICIES IMPLEMENTED FOR TRIBAL DEVELOPMENT IN INDIA

The brief understanding about tribal development in India in a chronological order can be understood by making a clear review about the efforts and impact of the Five-Year Plans on the scheduled tribes up till the Seventh Five Year Plan (1985-1989). From the Eighth Five Year Plan that marks its beginning in the year 1992, we shall discuss the major policies and programmes drafted and implemented by the Government of India for the upliftment of the tribes of the nation irrespective of the fact of its direct or indirect impact on the tribal communities.

3.5.1 FIRST FIVE YEAR PLAN (1951-1956)

The first five-year plan aimed to reconstruct the national economy along the lines of social equality. The major objective of this plan period was to bring about better and increased production along with an integrated change in the outlook of the tribal masses. Therefore, increase in the overall production alongside the decrease in the existing inequalities was the primary objective of the first five-year plan. By the year 1954, forty-three special multipurpose projects for tribal development schemes alongside the Community Development Programme was added to bring about an upliftment of the tribal communities of India. Realising the difficulty of sustaining such intensive programmes for the entire tribal area, by the year 1956, smaller blocks were evolved in the highest tribal concentration areas known as Tribal Development Blocks for which special programmes were implemented for addressing the needs of the tribal people. For properly understanding the micro level problems, many tribal institutes were set up in almost eight states in the first five-year plan. Education was given prime importance to for which special trainings were imparted to the teachers, special text books were prepared to address the tribal dialects. Special assistance of the government was provided by opening up numerous schools, hostels, ashram schools and the granting of scholarships. Besides education, agricultural improvement of the tribal areas was also focused upon by providing fertile and irrigated lands, high yielding variety seeds, bullocks, better financial aids with an aim to protect them from being exploited in the hands of the money lenders and the middlemen. Forest labour cooperatives were set up to assist and guard the tribal people from exploitation in the hands of the middlemen and exploiters of forest produce. During the first five-year plan, major emphasis was laid on education, economic development in the form of improvement of roads and infrastructures and on public health and medical facilities. Furthermore, skill development and vocational trainings were imparted to empower the tribal communities of the nation.

Special mention must be made about the Community Development Programme which was a form of Rural Tribal Extension Agency meant for transforming the social and economic life of the tribes and the areas that they live in. The community development programme aimed to encourage the participation of the common people in the developmental activities by utilizing the locally available resources. The main idea that lay behind the community development programme was to make a single multipurpose functionary responsible for all rural/ tribal development activities at the grass root level in order to meet the requirement of the rural/ tribal households especially in the field of agriculture. The initiation of the Special Multipurpose Tribal Blocks in the 1954-55 was the first systematically developed efforts for bringing about tribal development in India. Forty-three blocks of this kind were opened up in different states in 1956 to bring about a speedy process of development in the tribal concentrated areas. Besides, the Voluntary Organizations working for the welfare of the tribes financed by the State Government, Ministry of Home Affairs and the Ministry of Social Welfare also marked an important dimension of tribal development with special reference to the promotion of Tribal Development Programmes. These voluntary organizations generally worked in the areas of education, opening up of ashrams and hostels, medical aid and skill development through vocational training centres. Therefore, the first five-year plan basically focused upon the overall increase in economic production and the reduction of social inequality.

3.5.2 SECOND FIVE YEAR PLAN (1956-1961)

The Second Five Year Plan was formulated with the objective of a rapid increase in the national income in order to raise the standard of living of the countrymen by using the help of industrialization particularly in the sectors of basic and heavy industries and a large scale expansion of opportunities to bring about socio economic equality. The major step taken by the government in the second five-year plan towards the development of the tribal communities was the setting up of the Multipurpose Project Block with the ultimate aim of creating a progressive outlook in the economy and thereby achieving major developments in the material and cultural aspects of tribal life. Multipurpose pilot projects were established to bring about coordinated and intensive development in the tribal areas that was modified to address the tribal problems intricately. An evaluation of the multipurpose project blocks submitted by a committee headed by Verrier Elwin on Special Multipurpose Projects in 1960 led to a change in the third plan period in the form of starting up of the Tribal Development Blocks because the pilot projects were not free from loopholes. Several recommendations were made by the committee such as adoption of a more flexible approach towards allocation of funds in a systematic manner, reduction in the outlay of expenditure and the introduction of supervisory body in the form of the Panchayati Raj Institutions. Taking these recommendations into consideration, the Tribal Development Blocks Programmes were carved out of the Multipurpose Pilot projects and was implemented at the end of the project. During the second five-year plan, the government tried to accentuate the growth rate of tribal development by adding to the various already existing as well as the new policies and programmes designed for the development of the tribes of India in state wise manner. These supplementary programmes worked upon the areas such as cooperative farming through participative development which was transcended to the form of Khadi and Village Industries Programme (1957), Village Housing Projects Scheme (1957), Special Multi-Purpose Tribal Development Blocks Programme (SMTB) (1959), Panchayati Raj

(1959), Package Programme (1960), Intensive Agricultural District Programme (1960).

Therefore, it can be stated that during the second five year plan an effort was made to bring about development without disturbing the prevailing tribal culture and legacy on the lines of participative development with the ultimate aim of poverty alleviation, promotion of better standard of living through betterment in health facilities and other socio-economic equality programmes.

3.5.3 THE THIRD FIVE YEAR PLAN (1961-1966)

By the third five-year plan, it was made clear that the development of the tribes of India should be made in accordance to their own line of tradition and culture without pressuring them from outside interference. The major focus of the third five-year plan was on the administration of the grass roots through Panchayati Raj and its three tire models of democratic decentralization. In the tribal blocks, efforts were made to identify and sketch out programmes for the Tribal Development Blocks (TDP) (1961), Tribal Area Development Programmes (TADP) (1962), Hill Area Development Programmes (HADP) (1962), Intensive Agriculture Area Programme (IAAP) (1964), and Intensive Area Development Scheme (IADS) (1965). Special priority was given to the programmes on economic upliftment of the tribal people and the economic rehabilitation of the people engaged in shifting agriculture. In order to meet the credit requirements of the tribal agriculturists and artisans, special financial and other multi- purpose cooperatives were started. Special attention was given to the issues such as improvement in the quality of land, land reclamation, minor irrigation, soil conservation, improved high yielding variety of seed supply, fisheries, cattle, poultry and sheep breeding and vocational training for the artisans. Roads, culverts and bridges were constructed for connectivity of the villages to the urban areas as developmental projects. The health of the rural tribal people was focused upon specially the areas of female maternity, child welfare and the provision of hygienic drinking water to curb the water borne diseases. During the third five-year plan period, 489 Community Development Blocks housing more than 66% of tribal population were converted to Tribal Development Blocks where the Tribal Development Blocks Programmes were started off which was the intensification of the projects of the Community Development Blocks with a higher development of resources to take care of the tribal problems. Bordoloi, (1989). The third five-year plan covered three hundred Tribal Development Blocks which primarily worked in the areas such as planning, training coordination and the tribal rights on forests and land, productive channelization of the skills of the youths through the proper implementation of vocational training etc.

3.5.4 THE FOURTH FIVE YEAR PLAN (1969- 1974)

The principal objective of the fourth five-year plan was growth and stability along with the achievement of social equality. The problems of the scheduled castes and the scheduled tribes were enlisted specially in consultation with the studies of 1959 and 1969 and also the SC&ST Commission of 1961. It was realized that the individual welfare approach or the schematic block approach falls inadequate to solve the economic problems of the tribal people. Therefore, the formulation of individual plans for each level of development of a particular tribal area that suited their specific potentiality and the level of development marked to be of prime significance. From the year 1962 onwards, the Tribal Development Blocks became the chief patron of development for the tribal population. However, these Tribal Development programmes were not free from criticisms like the failure of the general sector in reaching to the everyday life of the tribal people and the sole upliftment of the creamy section of the tribal population leaving behind the majority grass root population who still remained closely knit in the vicious cycle of underdevelopment and misery. The Shilu Ao Committee in its report of 1969 furthermore pointed out that the programmes devised and implemented on the grass root tribal people did not suit the level of their development. Since it followed the top down approach the programmes were suitable for some other groups that stood higher on the ladder and scale of development. It was simply unrealistic to expect a positive outcome from an unsuited planned framework. It was pointed out that the employment generation schemes were not given due recognition and no concrete steps were taken to settle the land dispute problems. To sum up, it can be stated that the fragmented approach to tribal development at the block level proved to be one of the major loopholes in the proper outcome of the devised policy programmes for tribal development.

On a positive note, the major developmental activities undertaken during the Fourth Five Year Plan were the allotment of land scheme, grant of subsidies for the purchase of plough, bullocks and the schemes to develop agriculture via better seeds, soil conservation, animal husbandry schemes etc. The major programmes formulated during the Fourth Five Year Plan stand to be as follows: Tribal Area Development Programme (1972), Pilot Projects for Tribal

Development (1972), Pilot Intensive Rural Employment Project (1972), Employment Guarantee Scheme (1972), and the formation of the Tribal Development Blocks. The areas of development specifically categorized in the Fourth Five Year Plan were education, economic development and health and housing.

3.5.5 THE FIFTH FIVE YEAR PLAN (1974-1979)

'Removal of poverty and the attainment of self-reliance' was the main objective of the draft of the Fifth Five year Plan. The realization of this goal indicated the accomplishment of the higher growth rate, proper income distribution, and an increase in the rate of domestic savings and most important of all, improvement in the standard of living of the weaker and the poorer sections of the society. In this background, special attention was given to implement policies for the reduction of the gap between the tribe and the non tribe population of the country with the help of large investments and other suitable physical efforts to bring them to the national mainstream. The focus of attention of the Fifth Five Year Plan was on the introduction and understanding of the term 'Basic Minimum Needs' through Tribal Sub Plans and integrated Tribal Development Projects (1974), Tribal Development Projects (1975), Twenty Point Programme Antyodaya (1975), Antyodaya (1977), Comprehensive Area Development Programme (1978), Integrated Rural Development Programme (1979), Training of Rural youth for Self Employment (1978).

Taking into consideration the loopholes of the developmental policies for tribal development during the Fourth Five Year Plan, the Dube committee came out with some major rectifying suggestions in the Fifth Five Year Plan. The first one being that of an integrated approach to tribal development with a view to bridge the gap between the developmental level of the tribal and non tribal areas; while the second being the improvement in the quality of life of the tribal people. The National Planning Commission having understood the lopsided development policies towards the tribes came up with an integrated approach towards tribal development in the form of the launching of the Tribal Sub Plan which was endowed with the responsibility of eliminating exploitation by increasing the pace of development and an overall development in the organizational capacity. During the fifth Five Year Plan, through the Tribal Sub Plan, a serious emphasis was laid upon the building up of the infrastructure for the developmental purpose of the tribes of India. Projects on financial self-reliance such as development of horticulture, improved agriculture, fisheries, animal husbandry, small scale cottage industries were continued.

3.5.6 THE SIXTH FIVE YEAR PLAN. (1980-1985)

Bridging the gap between the tribal areas and the non tribal areas by accelerating the sub plan projects for tribal development happened to be the primary objective of the Sixth Five Year Plan. Under the tribal sub plan projects, the top most priority was given to the improvement of education in the tribal areas by the end of the Sixth Five Year Plan. The areas with 59% and above of tribal population were identified as Tribal Sub Plan Area where special attention was devoted to. During the Sixth Five Year Plan, the major focuses of attentions were four-fold in nature. Firstly, emphasis was laid on the provision of developmental services with a bottom up approach rather than the prevailing top down approach towards tribal development. Secondly, attempts were made to increase the employment level by the provision of diversified job opportunities and the imparting of the due training required to avail the beneficiaries the newly created job facilities. Special effort was made to bring about the coordination of the Special Micro projects and the working of the Integrated Tribal Development Agencies alongside the Tribal Sub Plan in order to improve the economic condition of the tribes with the target of making a visible increase of 50% of the tribal population above the BPL line by providing decent livelihoods in the form of improved agriculture, animal husbandry, horticulture and forestry. The government took strategic measures to curb the exploitation of the tribes in the hands of the middle men, money lenders by setting them free of unreasonable land tenure, bonded labour and debt. Large Sized Agricultural Multipurpose Societies commonly referred to as LAMPS were initiated in the tribal areas to bring about a responsible output in the infrastructural outgrowths. The primary focus of attention of the Sixth Five Year Plan was on the strengthening of the infrastructures in the tribal areas, the elimination of tribal (rural poverty) by the reduction of regional disparities with the help of Integrated Tribal Development Programmes. The backbone to these policies were provided by the following programmes- National Rural Employment Programme (1980), Prime Minister's New 20-point Programme (1980), Development of Women and Children in Rural Areas (DWCRA) (1983), Rural Landless Employment Guarantee Programme (1983), Programmes for Depressed Areas, Special Programmes for Women and Children, and Tribal Development Agency. For the pockets with tribal concentration with a minimum population of 10000 where at least half of the people belonging to the scheduled tribe communities, special programme was devised under the banner of Modified Area Development Approach.245

such MADA pockets were identified. Furthermore, the number of primitive tribes increased to seventy-two as twenty more tribal communities were identified and put under the banner of primitive tribes.

3.5.7 THE SEVENTH FIVE YEAR PLAN (1985-1990)

The Seventh Five Year Plan witnessed a substantial flow of funds for tribal development which led to an increase in the infrastructural facilities and the problem coverage areas not to forget the thrust being that of the educational development of the scheduled tribe communities. Two important institutions of the national level were set up for the economic development of the scheduled castes and the scheduled tribes namely- 1. Tribal Cooperative Marketing Development Federation (TRIFED) which was established in 1987 to function as an apex body for State Tribal Development Cooperative Corporations. 2. National Scheduled Castes and Scheduled Tribes Finance and Development Corporations (NSFDC) established in 1989. While the TRIFED was entrusted with the responsibility of providing remunerative price for the forest and agricultural produce of the tribal people, the NSFDC on the other hand was to facilitate employment generation by providing credit facilities. The Seventh Five Year plan looked into the measures to strengthen the anti-exploitation programmes, poverty alleviations programmes, and the socio- economic development programmes with the help of irrigation facilities, power generation and mining projects to up lift the socio- economic conditions of the tribes. The implementation of various legislatives measures specially in the field of agriculture like money lending, agricultural tenancy, bonded labour, forestry, excise, debt relief rehabilitation of the displaced population etc. to deliver social justice was an important landmark of the Seventh Five Year Plan. Active role of the Non-Governmental Organisations and Voluntary Organisations were witnessed to achieve the targets of an egalitarian society with socio economic stability and justice. To address the poverty problems of the tribal people, special emphasis was laid on the promotion of agriculture, horticulture, forestry, cottage industries and small scale industries, training on technical advancements, marketing and monetary advancements etc. Since the gap between the national educational level and that of the tribal educational level was seen to widen with the passage of time, the Seventh Plan paid due attention to the imparting of formal and vocational training to the tribal population. The major programmes that were implemented in this plan period were the Community Development Programme, Integrated Rural Development Programme, Rural Landless Employment Guarantee Programme (1983), Integrated Rural Energy Planning Programme, Jawahar Rozgar Yojana (1989). It can be stated that the Seventh Five Year Plan aimed to bring the tribal and non tribal population at par with each other by working on the upliftment of the former to be on an equal footing with the latter. In the achievement of this target the plan emphasized on the elimination of exploitation alongside tried to address some of the pertinent issues of land alienation, minimum wages and other human rights issues.

3.6 GOVERNMENT POLICIES POST 1990S

The chronological understanding of the policies and programmes charted out by the government has been provided in brief in the reviews of the five year plans up to the Seventh Five Year Plan

(1985-1990). The post liberalization era witnessed globalisation in the global political arena that touched upon the policies developed and designed for the tribes of India too. In this section, we intend to study some of the important policies and programmes implemented by the Government on the tribal population in the post liberalization era. The major challenge that is to be mentioned here is that it is almost impossible to analyse and narrate each and every policy of the post 1990s .Therefore, only those policies that are significant and relevant in bringing about tribal development have been highlighted. Furthermore, as has been pointed out earlier, there are two types of programmes helping in the development of the tribes. The first one being that which directly bring about development of the tribes and the second which is for an overall rural development that as well help the tribes in developing. Taking both the direct and indirect policies together, we shall present an overview of some of the major policies for tribal development from 1991 onwards compiling the efforts from the Eight Five Year Plan till the Twelfth Five Year Plan.

3.6.1 SUPPLY OF IMPROVED TOOL KITS TO RURAL ARTISANS (SITRA) 1992

The Supply of Improved Tool Kits to Rural Artisans was introduced in the year 1992 as a sub programme of the Integrated Rural Development Programme (IRDP) in some of the selected districts which gradually spread and covered all other districts of the country. The focus of attention of this programme was to enhance the quality of products of the artisans living below the poverty line by increasing their production and income. Under the scheme, artisans from different crafts living below the poverty line were to be given improved tools to enable them to enhance the quality/quantity/market potential of their products; the aim was also to prevent migration of the craftsmen to the urban areas and to enhance the living standards in rural areas of the poor. The findings of an independent research organization called the Development Alternatives, New Delhi, in its case studies of two districts of Agra and Aligarh have shown a positive impact of the SITRA on the artisans by increasing their income with the help of improved tool facilities. With the passage of time, this programme like the TRYSEM was merged with the Swarna Jayanti Gram Swarozgar Yojana (SGSY) in the year 1999.

3.6.2 RURAL SANITATION PROGRAMME (REVISED DURING 1992-93)

The Centrally sponsored Rural Sanitation Programme which was launched in 1986 was revised and made more effective during the years 1992-1993. This programme commonly referred to as the (CRSP) focused on the provisions of sanitary latrines to the Scheduled Caste and Scheduled Tribe families and also to those living under the poverty line. The financial responsibility of funding the programme was undertaken both by the centre and the state at a fifty percent ratio each. The revision and the revamping of the Rural Sanitation Programme was done during the year 1992-93 where it was decided that eighty percent of subsidy would be granted to the people living below the poverty level while the rest of the twenty percent would be taken up by the individual household. A special provision was made for the construction of exclusive sanitary complexes for women where the seventy percent of the cost would be contributed by the state and the central government and the rest of the thirty percent by the panchayats. The Rural Sanitary Marts (RSM), which happened to be the retail outlets were opened up for the purchase and easy distribution of the equipment of sanitary ware for the smooth operation of the above mentioned programme.

3.6.3 EMPLOYMENT ASSURANCE SCHEME (1993)

2nd of October, 1993, marks the starting of the implementation of the Employment Assurance Scheme (EAS) in the rural or tribal areas of 1778 tribal blocks of 261 districts. The EAS scheme aimed to provide an assured employment of 100 days of unskilled manual jobs to the rural poor in need of and seeking job opportunities. A minimum of 18 years and a maximum of 60 years stand to be the demarcating age group for both men and women, the residents of the rural blocks were covered under the EAS scheme. Not more than two adult members of a single family can be employed under the EAS scheme where more than 10 million people got registered themselves under the scheme by the year 1994. The centre and the state in a ratio of 80:20 share the financial burden of the Employment Assurance Scheme. The basic objective behind the introduction of the EAS scheme was to help the rural people during the lean season of agriculture by providing gainful employment in the form of manual or physical labour to the physically sound adults of the rural and tribal areas who are in need of work and are looking for one but have failed to find in the farm or other sectors. By fulfilling this primary objective, the secondary objective would be fulfilled within a due course of time. This being the achievement of the creation of economic infrastructure to bring about economic stability by adding to the community assets and a sustained employment and development facility.

3.6.4 PRIME MINISTER'S ROZGAR YOJANA (1993)

On the 2nd of October 1993, the then Indian Prime Minister formally announced the Prime Minister's Yojana which aimed to provide employment to the educated but unemployed people of the country. The educational qualification required was standard eighth passed. Earlier it was confined to the urban sectors, but from the year 1994, the scheme was extended to the rural as well as tribal areas alongside the urban areas of the nation. The provision of self employment to the educated unemployed persons in the agricultural sectors, village industries and small scale industries happened to be the primary focus of this scheme. The major focus of attention of this scheme was on the provision of employment to the educated unemployed youths and women with a target of reaching out to more than a million persons by setting up seven lakhs of micro enterprises for the educated unemployed youths. A loan up to 1 lakh for business and 2 lakhs for industrial and agricultural enterprises were advanced by the banks to the educated unemployed youths and straight away a sum of ten lakhs covered if two or more educated unemployed youths opt for partnership project under this scheme. The scheme coverered a reservation of 22.5% for the Scheduled Castes ad the Scheduled Tribes and 27% for the Other Backward Classes. It is the District Industry Centre that has the final say in the selection of the beneficiaries and the implementation of the employment programme.

3.6.5 TRAINING OF RURAL YOUTH FOR SELF EMPLOYMENT (TRYSEM)

The Year 1979 marks to be the foundation for the establishment of a significant programme called TRYSEM which was later on merged with the Swarna Jayanti Gram Swarozgar Yojana (SGSY) along with many other programmes such as IRDP, SITRA, Million Wells Scheme and the DWCRA in the year 1999. The Training of Rural Youth for Self Employment Programme commonly referred to as TRYSEM was formulate with the ultimate focus of providing the rural poor youths between the age group of 18- 35 years with the technical and entrepreneurial skills in order to enable them to start up some income generating activities in the form of self employment and wage employment. TRYSEM aimed to deliver training and technical skills to the rural youths out of which not less than fifty percent of them to belong to the Scheduled Caste and Scheduled Tribe communities and also net less than fifty percent from the women folk in a mandatory manner. 'There are no educational qualifications prescribed for the selection of trainees (Government of India, 1988:20-21).' The District Rural Development Agency decides on the selection of the syllabus of the TRYSEM programme and the managerial skills that include the basics of book keeping, basic knowledge of marketing and product costing, plan formulation and entrepreneurial assistance along with the familiarization with the banks for subsidies and loans. The major loopholes of the TRYSEM programme happen to be the lack of seriousness on the part of the people responsible of conducting the training thereby making the entire system a mere bunch of formalities. The mismanagement and the ill equipment of the training centres, nonpayment of the allotted stipends to the beneficiaries and the non issuance of the training certificated furthermore weakened the programme.

3.6.6 SWARNA JAYANTI GRAM SWAROZGAR YOJANA (SGSY) (1999)

The Swarna Jayanti Gram Swarozgar Yojana came into existence by merging out several different self employment programmes such as Integrated Rural Development Programme (IRDP), Training of Rural Youth for Self Employment (TRYSEM), Development of Women & Children in Rural Areas (DWCRA), Supply of Improved Toolkits to Rural Artisans (SITRA), and Ganga Kalyan Yojana (GKY) which were seen to be lacking in proper social intermediation and linkages within themselves. This programme was introduced by Prime Minister A.B. Vajpayee where the funding of the SGSY was to be done by the centre and the state at 75:25 ratios. The establishment of a large number of micro enterprises in rural areas to bring the poor families above the poverty line within a time span of three years with the help of the provision of income generating assets in the form of government subsidies and bank credits was the prime focus of attention of the SGSY programme. As a matter of fact, the SGSY is perceived as a holistic programme targeting the development of micro enterprises in the rural areas and the formation of Self Help Groups. For the promotion of a network of agencies such as the District Rural Development Agencies (DRDA), special importance was given to capacity building, support of infrastructures, credit, marketing and technology and the proper cluster formations. Emphasis was laid upon a proper network and communication facilities among the major stakeholders of development in the SGSY programme such as the DRDA in the State Governments, the NGOs, the Panchayati Raj Institutions and the banks. The SGSY programme categorically insists upon the idea that fifty percent of the Self Help Groups must be formed and operated exclusively by women and that fifty percent of the benefits should flow to the Scheduled Castes and the Scheduled Tribes. The Swarna Jayanti Gram Swarozgar Yojana (SGSY) has now been remodelled to form of the National Rural Livelihood Mission (NPLM) which is one of the largest missions of the world for the improvement of the livelihood of the poor.

3.6.7 JAWAHAR GRAM SAMRIDHI YOJANA (JGSY) 1999

With the ultimate objective of poverty alleviation at the village level, the Jawahar Gram Samridhi Yojana was launched in the year 1999 by A.V. Vajpayee. The programme focuses on the provision of maximum job opportunities and facilities to the poor villages for the creation of social assets. The funding to the JGSY was taken up by the centre and the state at 75:25 ratios.

The initiative for the provision of job opportunities especially to the rural poor primarily dependent on agriculture during the lean season began as early as the 1960s. To make this possible, several wage schemes were launched both by the centre and the state out of which the Jawahar Rozgar Yojana 1989 marked to be of the largest stature (because it was an amalgamation of many different likeminded programmes such as National Rural Employment Programme and the Rural Landless Employment Guarantee Programme.). This programme was redesigned in the year 1999 as the Jawahar Gram Samridhi Yojana (JGSY). To add to it, the JGSY aimed to create additional employment by creating productive assets. Later on, in the year 2001, the Employment Assurance Scheme and the Jawahar Gram Samridhi Yojana was integrated to form the Sampoorna Grameen Rozgar Yojana (SGRY).

3.6.8 FOOD FOR WORK PROGRAMME (2000-2001)

The Food for Work programme is one of the components of the Employment Assurance Scheme that was started off in the year 2000-01 in eight of the notified droughts affected states of Gujarat, Himachal Pradesh, Chhattisgarh, Madhya Pradesh, Orissa, Maharashtra, Uttaranchal and Rajasthan. The Food for Work Programme aims to provide food provision through wage employment where free of cost food grains are supplied to the state to facilitate the programme. However, the major loophole of this programme was the slow pace of lifting the food grains from the go downs of the Food Corporation of India which in turn hampered the overall distribution pattern thereby making the programme faulty and inefficient.

3.6.9 SAMPOORNA GRAMEEN ROZGAR YOJANA (SGRY) 2001

The merger of the Employment Assurance Scheme and Jawahar Gram Samridhi Yojana led to the launching of the Samporna Grameen Rozgar Yojana by A.B. Vajpayee in Sept 2001 with two major objectives of providing employment opportunities and food to the rural poor below the poverty line along with the provision of additional wage employment in the form of economic assets and infrastructure in the rural areas. The employments of the beneficiaries are done on temporary basis who are made to work on the construction of infrastructure and community assets. The target area of the programme was the upliftment of women, the Scheduled castes and the Scheduled Tribes of the rural zones where the financial burden of food distribution was shared both by the central and the state government, the execution of which was done by the three ties of Panchayati Raj System. The Samporna Grameen Rozgar Yojana was later on replaced by the National Rural Employment Guarantee Act 2005.

3.6.10 THE NATIONAL RURAL EMPLOYMENT GUARANTEE ACT (NREGA) 2005

The National Rural Employment Guarantee Act was launched by Dr. Manmohan Singh with the primary objective of providing one hundred days of guaranteed unskilled wage employment to one member of each rural household opting for it. It has been categorically stated here that all poor households irrespective of falling below or above the poverty level are entitled to the job scheme. This programme started on 2nd of February 2006 by covering two hundred districts which was extended to the entire nation within the time framework of 1st of April 2008 to 2nd of October 2009 whereby it was renamed as Mahatma Gandhi National Rural Employment Guarantee Act (MGNREGA). The programme works for the conservation of water resources, security measures from drought and flood, development of land and rural connectivity by constructing all weather roads. The day-to-day administration of this programme is bestowed in the hands of the Panchayati Raj system of the country that is responsible for the planning, implementation and monitoring with the Gram Sabha for the social auditing of the scheme. This scheme demands one third of its beneficiaries to be women and along with one fourth of the wage rate to be distributed in case of failure of the government to provide employment for the stipulated duration as unemployment allowance.

3.6.11 SPECIAL AREA DEVELOPMENT PROGRAMME 2007

It was in the Eleventh Five Year Plan that recognition was given to the fact that inclusive growth required more of its attention on the slow developing areas that are generally termed as the backward zones. The level of public investment must be increased in such areas to bring them to a common platform whereby the process of development would be aggravated extensively and the distribution of the fruits of development would be done in a just manner. Realizing this idea to the fullest and also understanding the fact that the pattern of development was lopsided in India, central government aided the state government by providing additional central assistance in the form of Backward Regions Grant Fund, Border Area Development Programme, the Hill Areas Development Programme/ Western Ghats Development Programme, Drought Prone Area Programme and the Tribal Area Development Programme. The major focus of attention would be the flow of development in the above specified areas to keep them abreast with the mainland development. Special mention must be made about the Integrated Tribal Development Agency which was specially formulated to narrow down the gap between the backwardness of the tribal areas with an intention to bring about a visible level of development in them. The method adopted to achieve this target was the elimination of corruption and exploitation in all forms, acceleration in the pace of socio-economic development level with the help of improving the organizational capacity within the tribal communities.

3.6.12 THE NATIONAL RURAL LIVELIHOOD MISSION (NPLM) (2011)

The then Prime Minister of India Dr. Manmohan Singh launched the National Rural Livelihood Mission in the year 2011 primarily designed for the alleviation of poverty by the year 2014-15. (The Hindu (Daily News Paper), Women Empowerment Schemes to take more time, July 7, 2009.p.11.). This programme was formulated by remodelling the Swarna Jayanti Gram Swarozgar Yojana and the responsibility of its implementation was handed over to the Ministry of Rural Development. This initiative is one of the world's largest poverty alleviation programme which is sponsored by the World Bank with a credit facility of one billion US Dollars. The main objective of the National Rural Livelihood Mission is to promote self employment and organization of the poor people of the rural areas with the help of the formation of Self Help Groups. Furthermore, the formation of women's Self Help Groups were encouraged by providing an interest subsidy of rupees one lakh to the poor households on the bank loans issued by them.

3.6.13 ADIVASI MAHILA SASHAKTIKARAN YOJANA (AMSY)

The Adivasi Mahila Sashaktikaran Yojana is a special programme exclusively designed for the welfare and development of the women belonging to the Scheduled Tribe communities. Under this scheme, the National Scheduled Tribes Finance and Development Cooperation is endowed with the responsibility of providing loans for various schemes and projects up to fifty thousand per individual or units. Furthermore, up to 90% of the cost of the scheme or the project is covered by the National Scheduled Tribes Finance and Development Cooperation.

3.6.14 PRADHAN MANTRI JAN DHAN YOJANA (PMJDY), 2014

The Pradhan Mantri Jan Dhan Yojana is a mission of national level launched by P.M. Narendra Modi to help enable an access to the financial services like banking facilities through the opening up of savings and deposit accounts and the utilization of credit, pension and insurance facilities. The Department of Financial Services, Ministry of Finance is endowed with the responsibility of ensuring a universal access to banking facility with at least one bank account for every household thereby generating financial literacy especially among people of the rural zones and backward areas.

3.6.15 TRIBAL SUB PLANS

The implementation of the Tribal Sub Plan was done during the Fifth Five Year Plan which marked a radical shift in the approach towards Tribal Development whereby the Scheduled Tribes would be directly benefitted. The Tribal Sub Plan can be regarded to be an umbrella term where all the schemes implemented by the state and the central government are brought together on a single platform for addressing the different needs of the Scheduled Tribe communities. The Tribal Sub Plan is basically an area based programme that focuses on the infrastructural development and family orientation of the Scheduled Tribes. The Ministry of Tribal Affairs apart from the state and central aid can take up developmental issues based on the improvement of infrastructure under Article 275(1) of the constitution. Financial assistance is granted to the state or the Union

Territory by the centre for construction of hostels and coaching institutions, research and training centres, ashrams and schools for the Scheduled Tribe students. Special mention must also be made about the Non-Governmental Organisations in the implementation of the TSP projects. The NSFDC and other related banks help with the financial matters with regard to the Tribal sub Plan.

The Tribal Cooperative Marketing Development Federation (TRIFED) was set up by the Government in the year 1987 with the prime objective of providing marketing assistance and remunerative prices to tribals for their Minor Forest Produce (MFP) and Surplus Agricultural Produce (SAP). The formation of the TRIFED also holds another significant reason that had grasped the ground level reality and also that which had acted as a curtailment in the growth rate of developmental activities of the tribal people. The areas to be addressed were the prevalent forms of exploitation of the tribes whose livelihood depended on the minor forest produce and corruption in case of the middlemen in between the tribes and the market. This organization acted as a smooth pathway connecting the people at the ground working as the collectors of minor forest produce and also the small marginal farmers and the market and also helped in fetching for the beneficiaries a decent income pattern/ remuneration free from corruption and exploitation.

Having studied some of the various important policies and programmes that are both directly and indirectly beneficial for the development of the Scheduled Tribes of India, the chapter would remain incomplete without highlighting on some of the recent measures taken up by the Ministry of Tribal Affairs as an effort of developing the Scheduled Tribes. These can be listed as below:

❖ **Special Central Assistance & Grants under Article 275 (1) of the Constitution.**

In order to supplement their efforts for the upliftment of the Scheduled Tribes through the Tribal Sub Plans, special central assistance is granted to the states and the Union Territories that basically targets the area of attention towards family oriented income generating schemes, soil conservation , water management, forest, education, animal husbandry, cooperatives, fisheries, small scale agriculture and industries etc. under the provision of Article 275(1); special grants are also given to the states and the Union Territories in order to meet the financial cost of the special projects designed for tribal welfare and also for the smooth functioning of the administration within the scheduled areas.

❖ **Schemes of Development of the Primitive Tribal Group (PTGs)**

Considering the vulnerability of the seventy five tribal groups under the primitive category, in the year 1998-99 a special Central Sector Scheme was devised for the all round development of this group. The scheme is very flexible, and covers housing, infrastructure development, education, health, land distribution/development, agriculture development, cattle development, social security, insurance, etc. During 2007-08, comprehensive long term "Conservation-cum-Development (CCD) Plans" for PTGs has been formulated for Eleventh Plan period through baseline surveys conducted by respective State

Governments/Union territory. These Plans envisage a synergy between efforts of State Governments and non-governmental organizations.

- **Tribal Research Institutes.**

In the states of Andhra Pradesh, Assam, Bihar, Gujarat, Kerela, Madhya Pradesh, Rajasthan, Orissa, Maharashtra, West Bengal, Tamil Nadu, Uttar Pradesh, Tripura and Manipur, fourteen Tribal Research Institutions have been established for the purpose of providing planning inputs to the government, conducting research, collection of data, evaluation of the studies conducted etc. Some of these research institutes also hold a museum for the promotion of tribal art and culture.

- **Vocational Training Centre in Tribal Areas.**

Apart from the setting up of hostels for both male and female Scheduled Tribe students and the Ashram schools, scholarships and coaching institutes in the Tribal Sub Plan areas, vocational training centres were opened up in the tribal areas with the ultimate aim of upgrading the vocational skills of the tribal youths in both the traditional and modern work culture depending upon their educational qualifications. The scheme provides 100% grant, and is implemented through State Governments, UT Administration and NGOs. The scheme prescribes fixed financial norms. However, no cost for the construction is provided.

3.7 MAJOR INSTITUTIONAL STRUCTURES FOR THE DEVELOPMENT OF THE SCHEDULED TRIBES

It can be rightly pointed out that both the Central and the State Governments have formulated a variety of different developmental agencies and the governmental departments with the ultimate aim of addressing the Scheduled Tribe issues. This study can be broadly taken up by throwing light on each of the endeavours of the federal structure of the Indian Union i.e. the central agencies and the state agencies.

3.7.1 CENTRAL GOVERNMENT

- **Ministry of Tribal Affairs**: The Ministry of Tribal Affairs is relatively a new ministry that was constituted in 1999 with the objective of 'providing more focused attention on the integrated socio-economic development of the most under-privileged sections of the Indian Society namely, the Scheduled Tribes in a coordinated and planned manner'. Hence, the responsibility for overall policy, planning and coordination of the developmental programmes of the Scheduled Tribes lie with the Ministry of Tribal Affairs by directly funding the Scheduled Tribe welfare.
- **National Commission for Scheduled Tribes**: The then existing National Commission for Scheduled Castes and Scheduled Tribes that was created in 1978 was bifurcated in 2004 by a constitutional amendment thereby leading to the birth of the National Commission for Scheduled Tribes (NCST) whose role is basically to monitor the measures for Scheduled Tribes welfare, investigate on the atrocities and violation of rights of the

Scheduled Tribes thereby suggesting special measures in order to safeguard the rights, livelihoods and the natural resources of the Scheduled Tribes.

- **Tribal Sub Plan/ Integrated Tribal Development Projects**: Post Fifth Five Year Plan has witnessed a change in the route of the development funds via a scheme known by the term Tribal Sub Plan (TSP), which was specially created for spending money in blocks housing more than 50 percent of its population as the Scheduled Tribes. The funds are to be spent through Integrated Tribal Development Agencies at the block level under the banner of Integrated Tribal Development Projects, thereby directly benefitting the Scheduled Tribe beneficiaries.

- **Commission for Scheduled Areas and Scheduled Tribes** – Article 339(1) of the Indian Constitution provides a Commission for Scheduled Areas and Scheduled Tribes which was set up for the first time in 1960 headed by U.N. Dhebar as Scheduled Areas and Scheduled Tribes Commission. Dilip Singh Bhuria headed the second Commission set up in 2002 that submitted its report to the President of India in 2004.

- **Committee on Welfare of Scheduled Castes and Scheduled Tribes** - This Committee is one of the three elected committees in Parliament which acts as a joint committee with twenty members from the Lok Sabha and ten members from the Rajya Sabha. This committee has been delegated the power to summon Government officials, demand reports with regard to the matters of Tribal Welfare etc.

- **National Scheduled Tribes Finance and Development Corporation (NSTFDC)** – This Central Government Financial Body was set up in 2001 for channelizing Central Funds towards Schemes for income generation, skill up-gradation, training and the procurement of minor forest produce.

- **Tribal Co-operative Marketing Development Federation (TRIFED)** - In many of the states of India, the State Governments have created Co-operatives for the purpose of marketing the products produced by the Scheduled Tribes especially those that are based on non-timber forest materials. Engaged in marketing development activities for Tribal products, the TRIFED is a national federation of the minor co-operative bodies.

3.7.2 STATE GOVERNMENT

- **Department of Tribal Welfare** – In most of the states with a significant Scheduled Tribe population, special separate departments and ministries are created for tribal welfare, while in those states where the Scheduled Tribes populations are not significant, the welfare policies are run under the control of the department of the backward classes (Dalits, Adivasis and Other Backward Castes). The Departments of Tribal Welfare look after the administration of the development schemes by channelizing funds to the concerned areas.

- **Tribal Advisory Council** – Paragraph 4 of the Fifth Schedule of the Indian Constitution states that 'every state with areas under that Schedule, or any other state whose Governor should so direct, must have a Tribes Advisory Council'. It is the Governor that appoints the members of the Council whose duty is to advise the former with regard to the functioning of the Fifth Schedule.

- **The Scheduled Areas:** The Constitution of India under two Schedules i.e. the Fifth and Sixth Schedules has made special arrangements for areas especially inhabited by the Scheduled Tribes.

- **The Fifth Schedule** – The Governors of states are conferred with some special powers and responsibilities under the provision of the Fifth Schedule to the constitution. The Fifth Schedule defines Scheduled Areas to be such areas as the President, by order may declare to be Scheduled Areas post consultation with the Governor of that state and in the State Government. Preponderance of Tribal population, compactness and reasonable size of the area, a viable administrative entity such as a district, block or taluk, economic backwardness of the area are the special criteria for declaring any area as a Scheduled Area under the Fifth Schedule. Some of the noteworthy provisions in the Scheduled Areas for the benefit of the tribals stand to be as follows:

  The Governor of a state having Scheduled Areas can make regulations to i. Prohibit or restrict transfer of land from tribals; ii. Regulate the business of money lending to the members of the Scheduled Tribes; iii. Make a report to the President regarding the administration of the Scheduled Areas in the state; iv. Establish a Tribal Advisory Council in states having Scheduled Areas; **v.** Look into the Panchayats Extension to Scheduled Areas (PESA) (Act 1996) under which the provisions pertaining to Panchayats or elected village councils, are extended to the

Scheduled Areas that contain special benefits for the Scheduled Tribes.

- **The Sixth Schedule** – The administration of certain Tribal Areas in the states of Assam, Meghalaya, Tripura and Mizoram are guided by the constitution under the Sixth Schedule governed by Autonomous District and Autonomous Regions under Article 244(2). The District Councils, Autonomous Councils and Regional Councils with the approval of the Governor are empowered to make rules with regard to areas such as dispensaries, markets, primary schools, fisheries, waterways, roads and roads transports. Except for Bodoland and Tripura, the Autonomous Council under the Civil Procedure Code and Criminal Procedure Code have been conferred the powers to try certain suits and offences, to collect revenues and regulate and manage the natural resources not touching upon the areas of the reserved forests and land acquisition by the State Government. The Supreme Court had made it clear that the powers of the councils are specifically limited to the subjects specified in the Sixth Schedule and cannot infringe upon power areas such as land transfers, and non-timber forest produce royalties. *(District Council of United Khasi and Jaintia Hills and Ors .Etc. vs. Sitimon Sawian Etc, 1 SCR 398).*

3.8 GOVERNMENTAL POLICIES POST 2014

The policies on tribal development have witnessed a gradual change with the change in the central government that make an attempt to mould the existing policies conducive to their party affiliations, election manifesto and political ideology. The change witnessed in the policies of tribal development after the 1990s with the advocacy of liberalization in the nation has definitely marked a change in the existing policies towards the development of the scheduled tribes, laying more emphasis upon the quality of human life. 27th of May 2014, marks the coming in of a new set of policy formulators and administrators with a change in the central government. Prime Minister Narendra Modi and his ministry are well known for the drastic changes in the existing method of governance. The replacement of the National Planning Commission by the NITI Aayog that would be working on the lines of bottom-up approach as perceived by the ministry, speaks for itself aloud. The speeches delivered by the Prime Minister and his cabinet on the upliftment of the backward communities and the scheduled tribes make us believe about his intentions to work for tribal development on dedicated lines. However, to review the functioning of the present government on tribal development would be too early and an amateur task to conduct. Yet, we would like to draw the attentions of the readers on some of the important policies adopted and upgraded by the present government for tribal development since the year 2014.

The year ending review of 2017 provided by the Ministry of Tribal Affairs highlights on the twelve major areas that have been developed in the due course of tribal development. Some of the noteworthy areas that need a mention stand to be as follows:

- **Socio Economic Development**

  The socio-economic development of Scheduled Tribes (STs) through especially tailored education, infrastructure and livelihood schemes to fill in for critical gaps. Allocation of Business Rules (ABR) of the Government now mandates this Ministry to monitor 'Tribal Sub-Plan' (now called as 'Scheduled Tribe Component') funds of Central Ministries based on the framework and mechanism designed by NITI Aayog.

❖ Budget allocation for Minor Projects

The Budget allocation for the Ministry of Tribal Affairs has gone up from Rs. 4827.00 Cr in the year 2016-17 to Rs. 5329.00 Cr in 2017-18. Also, allocation for the welfare of Scheduled Tribes across all Ministries has witnessed an increase from Rs. 24005 Cr in the year 2016-17 has gone up to Rs. 31920 Cr in the corresponding period. The Ministry has already utilized 70% of its allocated outlay on various developmental initiatives for STs. An amount of Rs. 2280.49 Cr (as on 21st December, 2017) has been released under two Special Areas Programme of the Ministry viz. Special Central Assistance to Tribal Sub-Scheme and Grants under Article 275(1) of the Constitution for Education, Health, Livelihood /Income Generation Activities etc.

❖ Monitoring of funds for tribal development

There are 32 Central Ministries and Departments having 'Tribal Sub-Plan (TSP)' funds [now called as 'Scheduled Tribe Component'(STC)] catering to specific tribal development in various sectors through 273 different schemes.

Allocation of Business Rules (ABR) has been amended in January, 2017 whereby Ministry of Tribal Affairs (MoTA) has been given mandate for monitoring of STC funds of

Central Ministries based on the framework and mechanism designed by NITI Aayog. An online monitoring system has been put in place with web address stcmis.nic.in. The framework envisages monitoring of allocations for welfare of STs under the schemes, monitoring of expenditure vis-à-vis allocations, monitoring of physical performance and outcome monitoring. The framework also envisages to capture location wise details to ensure accountability and targeted spending.

❖ **Skill Development**

An amount of Rs. 165 Crore has been released to various states under the scheme Special Central Assistance to Tribal Sub-Scheme (SCA to TSS) and Grants under Article 275(1) for skill development of more than 71 thousand male and female tribal beneficiaries in a wide gamut of trades such as (i) Office Management (ii) Solar Technician / Electrician (iii) Beautician (iv) Handicraft (v) Skills required for day to day construction works (such as Plumbing, Mason, Electrician, Fitter, Welder, Carpenter (vi) Refrigeration and A/C repairing (vii) Mobile repairing (viii) Nutrition (x) Ayurvedic & tribal medicines (xi) IT (xii) Data Entry (xiii) Fabrication (xiv) Paramedics and Home Nurse Training (xv) Automobile Driving and Mechanics (xvi) Electric & Motor Winding (xvii) Security Guard (xviii) Housekeeping & Management (xix) Retail Management (xx) Hospitality (xxi) Eco-tourism (xxii) Adventure Tourism.

- **Construction of Museums of Tribal Freedom Fighters**

  The Government shall work to construct tribal museums in different states so that the coming generations may know how our tribals were far ahead in making sacrifices. Ministry has decided to construct a state-of-the-art Tribal Museum of national importance in Gujarat with a total cost of Rs. 75.00 Crore out of which Ministry of Tribal Affairs will provide Rs. 50.00 Crore. An amount of Rs. 25.00 Crore has already been released to the State.

- **Initiatives under Particularly Vulnerable Tribal Groups (PVTGs)**

  Ministry has enhanced the allocation of funds for the development of particularly Vulnerable Tribal Groups (PVTGs) from Rs. 270 crores in 2016-17 to Rs. 340 crores in 2017-18.

  State Governments have been given the flexibility of utilizing the funds using the gaps identified through the Survey.

  In order to ensure the overall and particular development of PVTGs, emphasis is being given on Micro planning using GIS mapping of tribes. Emphasis in the Comprehensive cum Development (CCD) is for preserving traditional architecture, traditional medical practices and cuisine and maintaining the heritage and culture of PVTGs.

- **Scholarships**

  The government has allocated funds, keeping in view the necessity and importance of education and has offered different types of scholarships to the students in the form of pre-matric, post-matric, scholarships for higher education etc.

- **Aadi Mahotsav**

Ministry of Tribal Affairs in association with TRIFED had organized a National Tribal Festival from 16th November, 2017 to 30th November, 2017. The festival commenced with a tribute to Birsa Munda, legendary tribal leader, freedom fighter and folk hero on his 142nd birth anniversary through an advertisement in print and social media on 15th November, 2017.

- **NGO Grants**

Ministry has been funding NGOs in service deficient areas in sectors such as Health, Education etc. In order to ensure transparency and in line with Government policies, NGO Grants portal has been developed. Henceforth, all interventions will be funded through applications received only through online portal. Also new projects on merits will be considered for funding after many years.

- **Minimum Support Price for Minor Forest Produce**

The MSP for the ten MFP items which had formed a part of the scheme since inception in 2013-14 had been revised on 31.10.2016. Also, furthermore MFP items had been included in the list of MFP items and the scheme was made applicable all over the country. Prior to that the Scheme was applicable only in Schedule V States. Subsequently, the MSP of the ten items existing in the Scheme since its inception were further reviewed consequent upon a study conducted by M/s TERI, Delhi on behest of TRIFED, and recommendation of the Pricing Cell. The MSP of five items viz. Sal Seed, Sal Leaves, Chironji Pods with seeds, Rangeeni Lac and Kusumi Lac have been increased in November, 2017.

Apart from the above mentioned major areas of tribal development, the present government intends to bring about a convergence of multiple programmes parallel to each other so as to achieve the desired target of development. Let us observe some of the major governmental efforts for tribal development through the process of convergence model.

- **Van Bandhu Kalyan Yojana (VKY):**

To create high quality social and physical infrastructure in an accelerated manner through strategic interventions to bridge the gap in the Human Development Index and to reap untapped potential of the Scheduled Tribes communities, the Central Government has announced a strategic process "Van Bandhu Kalyan Yojana (VKY)" by re-engineering processes of existing interventions with focus on quality education, health, livelihood development, infrastructure development without compromising cultural identity of Scheduled Tribes during the budget session of the Parliament on 10th July 2014. Van Bandhu Kalyan Yojana, mainly focuses on the integrated, holistic and inclusive development of tribal communities in core areas of education, health, livelihood, housing, drinking water, irrigation, access to basic facilities, institutions, cultural heritage, security and sports. Introduced by the Central government in 2014 as a Central Sector Scheme with an allocation of Rs. 100 crore.

The Central Government proposes to replicate the intervention with special focus on

- the qualitative and sustainable employment for tribal families;
- bridging infrastructure gaps with focus on quality;
- Improving the quality of education and health and improving the quality of life in tribal areas.

The major area of attention of this programme is to bring about qualitative and sustainable employment, emphasis on quality education & higher education, accelerated economic development of tribal areas, health for all, housing for all, safe drinking water for all at doorsteps, irrigation facilities suited to the terrain, all weather roads with connectivity to the nearby town/cities, universal availability of electricity, urban development, robust institutional mechanism to roll the vehicle of development with sustainability, Promotion and conservation of tribal cultural heritage and promotion of Sports in tribal areas.

The scheme been launched on pilot basis in one block each of the (10 Schedule V) States of AP, MP, HP, Telangana, Orissa, Jharkhand, Chhattisgarh, Rajasthan, Maharashtra and Gujarat.

Under the scheme centre will provide Rs. 10 crores for each block (total Rs. 100 crores for 10 blocks) for the development of various facilities for the Tribals. These blocks have been selected on the recommendations of the concerned States and have very low literacy rate.

- **Model Blocks:**

  There are about 350 Blocks in the Schedule V areas where population to STs compared to total population of the Block is 50% or above. Despite several interventions in the past, these Blocks are still reeling under various facets of deprivation in so far as Human Development Indices are concerned. Through VKY, it is envisaged to develop these Blocks as model Blocks over the period of next five years with qualitative and visible infrastructural facilities.

  The selection of block will be made in consultation with the respective State Governments while taking into account the human development indices.

- **Single Window System for Obtaining Market Information On Minor Forest Produces:**

  A Single Window System for obtaining information on Minor Forest Produces (MFPS) through Toll Free Call Service number 1800-180-1551 has been inaugurated where market rates information can be provided over phone to tribals and others on asking.

- **Synergy between two government bodies for infrastructure:**

  Establishing Toll Free Call Centre's would have entailed major capital and recurring manpower expenses. Hence,

TRIFED initiated a dialogue with Ministry of Agriculture (MOA) which is already running Kisan Call Centres (KCC) for disseminating market information about agricultural products. So, it was decided that instead of establishing a parallel infrastructure for similar service, TRIFED should leverage the existing infrastructure of Kisan Call Centres (KCC). Ministry of Agriculture agreed to provide the necessary linkage of "MFP net" with KCC. This is a commendable initiative of convergence between two bodies which has created synergy and optimum utilization of Govt. resources which will prove to be a trend setter for others. All the stakeholders of this service are benefitted with this convergence between two Ministries.

With the operationalisation of this service, tribals can call from anywhere and enquire about:MSP of different items, State Implementing Agencies for MSP for MFP, Market price of MFPs in different Markets, Dual advantage of KCC.

- **MFPNET Portal of TRIFED**:

The new MFPNET portal of Tribal Co-operative Marketing Development Federation of India (TRIFED) is designed to act as an adjunct and a catalyst for implementing the scheme of Minimum Support Price (MSP) for Minor Forest Produce (MFP). It is a one stop destination for all information needed on MFPs and facilitates stakeholders in MFP trade and users to take decisions backed by requisite information. It is a platform to collect and disseminate MFP trade related information and latest developments in this field. The information shall be available commodity wise and state wise for different markets.

The main objective is to ensure fair price to MFP gatherers who are mainly tribals, enhance their income level and ensure sustainable harvesting of MFPs. It is initially implemented for 10 main identified MFPs in 102 districts of 8 States. It is expected to increase quantum of MFP procurement substantially thereby benefitting tribal people. The Scheme also envisages training of 1,00,000 MFP gatherers of tribal origin on sustainable harvesting and value addition activities. This portal provides information about TRIFED, MFP trade in India, marketing prospects for MFPs, MSP for MFP, its current status, MFP development training beside its retail marketing activities.

Moreover, the portal is a network of stakeholders in the trade of MFP which includes individuals, agencies and institutions. Emails & SMSs about daily market prices shall be sent to all those interested in knowing the market prices and registered with the MFP net. In addition, MFP net also has the provision to upload information on buying and selling. Buyers and sellers can upload the trade leads about the MFP stock they want to sell or buy directly and the same shall be visible to all other visitors on the site. The buyer/seller interested to pursue these trade leads can get in touch with each other directly.

- **Other initiatives:**

  The government has given in-principal approval for recognizing the Vishva Bharati, Shanti Niketan as the other centre of excellence in the field of Tribal language and literature. A proposal to establish a National Research Centre in the Tribal Research Institute, Bhubaneshwar to promote research activities on subjects/issues for socio-economic development and culture of States has also been approved by the Government.

The guidelines provided by the present government for the development of the scheduled tribes definitely marks to be something with a positive dimension, but as mentioned earlier, to make an assessment at this initial phase may lead us to some faulty conclusions. However, it can be apparently stated that the policies for tribal development have definitely changed its directions from the top-down model to participatory bottom-up approach which has been the chief reason for the formation of the NITI Aayog in January 2015. The present government advocates about the inclusion of the marginalized and the scheduled tribes in the decision-making process through participation of the beneficiaries by creating new opportunities of development. This, however, can be substantiated only after the results of such policies on tribal development are obtained on the successful completion of such policies. Therefore, one can safely leave it open for time to decide on the success or failure of the above-mentioned policies for tribal development adopted by the existing government in question.

CHAPTER FOUR

Alternate Agencies of Tribal Development in India

4.1 UNDERSTANDING THE NON-GOVERNMENTAL ORGANIZATIONS

A Non-Governmental Organization is such an organization that is based upon non-profit motives that are generally free of governmental and international organizations in its functioning. Non-governmental organizations are known by different nomenclatures, such as, voluntary agencies, not-for profit organizations, civil society organizations, community-based organizations, charitable organizations, the third sector organizations and the like. Depending upon the nature of activities that such organizations undertake, the forms of non-governmental organizations also vary accordingly. Some of the different varieties of NGOs stand to be as follows –

i. Advocacy NGOs that campaign for specific issues.

ii. Consultancy/ research organizations that work for social and developmental activities.

iii. Training and capacity building organizations that focus only on the capacity building activities of target communities and other NGOs.

iv. Networking NGOs that create network opportunities for other NGOs in specific fields.

v. Mother NGOs that work as fund raisers and distributive agencies, clearing house, evaluator and encourage participation of NGOs for some specific projects.

vi. Grass roots organizations that work directly with the under privileged target communities.

vii. Self-help groups that work for the benefit of specific groups like women.

viii. Religious NGOs that work as the protagonist and protectors of some religious ideas.

ix. City based organizations whose work and activities are confined to the cities alone.

x. National organizations which are the NGOs bearing national character and presence.

xi. International organizations which have international linkages that basically performs the function of receiving and disbursement of grants to other such NGOs.www.indianngos.com/ngosection.htm, (2015)

Most of the non-governmental organizations are funded by international donations while some are run on the charity of the volunteers. NGOs are highly diverse groups of organizations engaged in a wide range of activities, and take different forms in different parts of the world. Some may have charitable status, while others may be registered for tax exemption based on recognition of social purposes. Others may be fronts for political, religious, or other interests.

Defining a non-governmental organization is a difficult task because the term NGO does not have a constrained scope of utility which therefore finds its applicability in different dimensions of its functioning thereby carrying a wide scope in its definition. The Indian Express in its edition of 1st August, 2015 stated that there are thirty-one lakh NGOs in India which happens to be more than double the number of schools in the country, 250 times the number of government hospitals, one NGO for 400 people as against one policeman for 709 people. This information was collected by the CBI from all the states (excluding Karnataka, Odisha and Telangana) and union territories on the basis of their registration in the Societies Registration Act. (*http://indianexpress.com*)

It is important to understand the institution of the non-governmental sector (NGOs) whose role in the public service framework has seen to be increasing specially in the areas of health, education and rural development. Campaigning and advocacy for the grass-root development within public policy at local and international levels have been the major tools in the growth of the non-governmental sectors. It has been seen that the government alongside the non-governmental organizations have started working together as partners for achieving the goal of all round development by complimenting on each other efforts. The term "NGO includes many different types of organizations from small local groups operating on a largely voluntary and informal basis, to large private development agencies with multi-million dollar budgets and thousands of paid professional staff". Lewis, (2008). In simple words, NGOs can be defined as "special governing, private, not-for profit organizations that are geared to improving the quality of life for disadvantaged people." Vakil, (1997). It can be rightly pointed out that the number and profile of NGOs has witnessed a rapid growth in the past decade both in the developed zone of the North characterized by high level of industrialization with the ultimate concern of the NGOs on poverty and social justice, and the lesser developed South where the NGOs play the role of potential partners along with the government for bringing about development. The importance of non-governmental organizations has increased manifold so much so to the extent of conceptualizing it as the *third sector* of institutions, a *voluntary sector* of uncoerced action and as a *civil society* for upholding the dignity of the citizens.

4.2 DELINEATING NGOS FROM VOLUNTARY ORGANISATIONS

"The term NGO (Non-Governmental Organization) seems to be deceptively simple. It may overlook the enormous variety and differential capabilities of NGOs. In fact, NGOs offer a Kaleidoscopic collection of organizations, varying in origin, size, programmes, ideology and control." Jha & Mishra, (2008). In understanding the meaning of the NGOs, we need to address the philosophy, programme, policy, role, funding, strategy, management and its evaluation to have a clear vision of it because parametrizing it on a single platform would give a mistaken overview of the subject. Originally, voluntarism was the chief doctrine behind the formation of the Non-Governmental Organizations that existed with the sole principle of surviving at its free will and action. Such voluntary efforts of providing services to the needy existed independent of the state. To throw light on the meaning of voluntary organization,

Stephen Hatch (1980) in his work *Outside the State* provides a few important characteristics that define and differ it from other organizations which stands to be as follows – i. The non-payment of participants is a character of many voluntary organizations which are typically not shared by commercial organizations; ii. With regard to the objective of the voluntary organizations, it can be argued that the VOs are all to some degree charitable which otherwise is not the objective of other such organizations; iii. In the formation of a voluntary organization no such statutes and enactments are required thereby making it an independent organization. However, in case of other profit-making association it is very important for it to find a place inside a governmental statute; iv. The aim of a voluntary organization is never on the lines of profit maximization and is therefore dependent and satisfied with private fees thereby making it completely different from the profit-oriented organizations; v. With regard to the behaviours of the voluntary organization, its major striking feature happens to be the nature of the organization, commitment of the organization and the involvement of the participants in accomplishing a non-profit task to the best of their abilities which places it a class ahead of the other organizations; vi. The size of the voluntary organizations is comparatively much smaller – generally comprising up of a nucleus and twenty participants while the other organizations have a much large size. Thus, these are the chief characteristic features of voluntary organizations as suggested by Hatch. However, after having studied Hatches' work, to place the typical NGOs working in the Indian context under the banner of voluntary organizations would problematize the subject on technical grounds. This is because when we study the non-governmental organizations on the above lines then it has some sharp contrasts to the very essence of voluntarism as provided by Stephen Hatch. However, under informal grounds and from a layman's point of view, the two terms i.e. the non-governmental organizations and the voluntary organizations are used interchangeably. D.C. Korten (1990) firmly believes that over the years, the functions of the voluntary development organizations have changed to i. Relief and welfare; ii. Community development; iii. Sustainable development and iv. People's movement. However, scholars like Cernea (1988) states that voluntarism in association are a key to all NGOs.

4.3 CHANGING DIMENSIONS OF THE NGOS

There has been a massive growth in the number and size of the non-governmental organizations in India especially after the adoption of the LPG or the Liberalisation, Privatization and Globalisation policies. In recent years, massive changes have been witnessed in the non-governmental sector leading to both its criticism and acclamation for its behaviour and functioning. In the areas where a diversity of population is present a common idea or an agreement on a particular issue is hard to achieve – be it the functioning of the state policies or the non-profit organizations. In such a situation the non-governmental organizations have definitely provided an alternative mechanism for proper services to the grass-root level (especially in the areas of health, education and empowerment). The World Development Report (1991), points out the importance of the non-governmental organizations by looking into "their ability to involve communities and grass-root organizations more effectively in the development process in addressing poverty." 'The current policy climate arguably requires NGOs to play the role of innovator more than ever in order to find real relevance in addressing issues of poverty, inequality and social change'. Lewis & Ravichandran, (2008).

There are multiple theoretical considerations that have supported as well as criticized the functioning of the NGOs in achieving the welfare of the marginalized grass-root communities. Ravishankar Kumar Singh (2003) in his work *role of NGOs in Socio-Economic Development* has listed the following significant *operational advantages of the non-governmental organizations* in the context of development –

- Due to the small and informal organization of the non-governmental organizations, it becomes very easy on their part to respond to the need of the hour and opportunities on humanitarian and developmental grounds within a short time span.
- NGOs can provide grass-roots services and dynamism in the remote areas inhabited by the poor communities where the developmental agencies and the government find it difficult to reach and work on. Robertson, (1989).
- The non-governmental organizations are seen to be more responsive to the social, cultural and other aspects of development that generally stands to be ignored by the technical development specialists.
- The considerable experiences of the NGOs in supporting the projects, strategies and programmes for both the urban and rural poor sections have earned them another feather in their hat.

- The non-governmental organizations fulfill to major roles of identifying the need of the community and mobilizing a broad and active participation to bring about support for the development at the local levels.
- Besides, the non-governmental organizations portray a willingness to initiate new approaches, techniques and experiments for development that may be of significance in the broader context.
- The operation and fulfillment of any particular project can be undertaken by a non-governmental organization at comparatively much lower cost than the governmental sector because the NGOs have a strong unit of low overhead, volunteers and workers that provide their services at a much lower cost thereby making the best out of the available resources.
- After having discussed the advantages of the non-governmental organizations it is very important for us to understand the *operational disadvantages* that it carries along with itself that can be listed as follows –
- Due to the diverse variety of the non-governmental organizations clubbed together by its comparatively small scale, size and burdened by unrealistic aims and operational activities, it is seen that many of the non-governmental organizations in fulfilling its developmental roles find it extremely difficult to collaborate with the other agencies and organizations of development.

- The problem of weak management of the non-governmental organizations because of its informal and voluntary nature and the scarce resources generally lead to a lack of control over operations and the limited accountability for funds.
- Due to the presence of individual efforts alone without a broader strategy, working relationship with other institutions and long-term focus, the functioning of the non-governmental organizations is severely hampered.
- Some of the non-governmental organizations operate on religious and political lines with its objectives not matching with that of the government and other development organizations leads to a massive hamper in the functioning of the organization.
- It has been seen that some of the NGOs drift away from their voluntary and participatory spirit, flexibility, independence and innovation which acts as a serious loophole.

David Korten (1990), in his study *from Relief to Peoples Movements* has classified the pattern of evaluation of NGOs under four generations namely –

- First generation – Relief and Welfare
- Second generation – Community Development
- Third generation – Sustainable Development
- Fourth generation – Peoples Movement

Diwakar Chand (1991) has classified the non-governmental organizations into three levels on the basis of its size –

- Local level NGOs with a minimum of 21 regular members.
- Regional level NGOs with a minimum of 151 regular members.
- National level NGOs with a minimum of 501 regular members.

4.4 NATURE & TYPES OF NON-GOVERNMENTAL ORGANIZATIONS

The meaning, dimension and nature of the non-governmental organizations have undergone a massive change with the change in time. As has already been discussed in the earlier chapters that development is a dynamic change-oriented subject and that both the government and the non-governmental organizations work for developmental purposes especially in the developing countries; this proves it enough to support the former argument. As the role of the government has changed from policing (vigilance) to welfare, so has the role of the NGOs changed from policy implementers to agencies of self-reliance. Not to forget the historical origin of the NGOs in the Indian context as voluntary organizations, with the advent of state, society and civilized life the nature of the NGOs has also witnessed change. Today, to what extent is a non-governmental organization a voluntary organization is left open to the scholars to debate on. With regard to the philosophy and purpose of the NGOs, C. Venkataiah (2009) states that "they come to carry out the social service oriented or development oriented functions; regarding their programmes are concerned they may perform single programme or variety of programmes (2009)." The non-governmental organizations on the basis of their typology may be compartmentalized into two broad categories **i.** Foreign/inter-governmental agencies and **ii.** National voluntary agencies. The national non-governmental organizations can be sub-divided into two groups – i. The institutional sector and ii. The people sector. Under the institutional sector, the groups of NGOs that work are business houses, religious group and local groups of foreign NGOs. Under the people/individual based sector, NGOs are basically i. service oriented, ii. Development oriented and iii. Action oriented. Furthermore, the action oriented groups are further divided into i. local people based NGO, ii. Field Staff based NGO and iii. Social action based NGO. Sashi Ranjan Pandey, (1991).

V.D. Deshpandey (1986) states that 'for carrying out the activities , voluntary agencies pool up financial resources either from their own source or from general public, donors (internal, and external-foreign) and from government. It is but natural that for extending financial asistance the governments, both central and state, generally recognise such NGOs which are legal entities, whose activities are open to all citizens irrespective of religion, caste, creed, sex or race; which are not specially for the benefit of any particular individual or community other than women, SC/ST and backward communities; and which are working in an area not included under any corporation, municipality, notified area committee of town or panchayat.'

The following chart will help us understand better the different typologies of the non-governmental organizations.

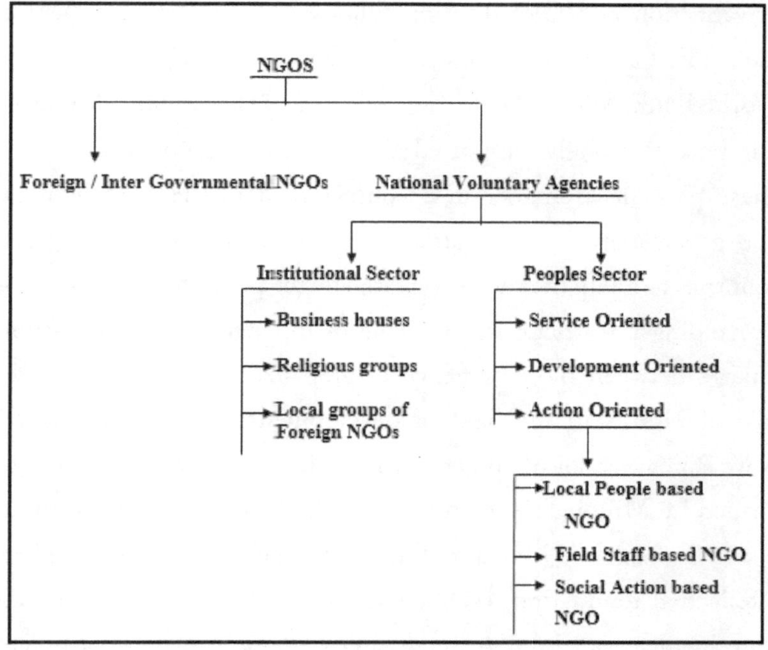

After having closely analysed the nature of the non-governmental organizations, we now proceed to the understanding of the NGOs at the global and national level, from the lense of the Indian prespective.

4.5 THE NON-GOVERNMENTAL ORGANIZATIONS ON A GLOBAL FORUM

The existence of social work on voluntary basis is a universal phenomenon that cannot be confined to any single country or a particular region but is instead entangled with human habitation from the ancient era. However, the tone and tenor of voluntarism have seriously changed with time where helping the helpless and the destitute have been replaced by structural reform measures especially in the socio-economic spheres. The era of (LPG) – Liberalization,

Privatization and Globalization followed by the establishment of the United Nations Organization alongside its agencies like the World Bank, World Trade Organization, International Monetary Fund have strongly supported the agenda of globalization. This phase particularly marks an encouragement in the growth of the non-governmental organizations particularly in the Third World countries to fill up the vacuum created by the policies of liberalization demanding a restriction in the role of the state. There is a strong linkage between the emergence of globalization and an increased role of NGOs in the field of development. This is because the New Right School of thought, the Chicago School of Economics headed by Milton Friedman and the Public Choice theorist under James Buchanan (1975) and William Niskanen (1971) who laid the intellectual foundation for liberalization and maintained that, 'the state involvement leads to increasing monopoly, increasing budget and suppressing of entrepreneurial behaviour, limiting choice, over production of unwanted services and encouragement to waste and inefficacy.' Gary & Jenkins, (1995). The World Bank Report of 2000-01 suggests that accelerated poverty reduction will require faster growth which in turn demands liberalization.

In the due process of globalization, the global actors in the form of International Government Organizations, the World Bank, International Monetary Fund and the World Trade Organization have started exercising more power and influence as compared to the rest of the actors because globalization itself advocates an increased accessibility to opportunities, borderless countries, more freedom, individualism, plural democracy and free enterprise. Therefore, in such a situation the NGOs are used as agents of change and development in order to promote capital formation alongside capital accumulation in the lesser developed countries. In order to curtail the negative effects of globalization the emergence of strong Civil Society movements and the non-governmental organizations are very important. R.K. Sapru (1998) in his monumental work *Development Administration: Crisis and Continuities* (1998) puts forward two major arguments in support of the non-governmental organizations/ civil society organizations. The first being failure of "market oriented economic development to protect some segments of society from abject poverty" and second being the possibility of "excessive government intervention leading to counterproductive in practice". Sapru suggests the development of partnership between the private sector and the non-governmental organizations in the implementation of developmental projects, policies and programmes so as to balance the weaknesses and strengths of these two mega sectors.

Although, the idea of global civil society traces its origin to the very recent 1990's, it is interesting to note the fact that serious efforts in order to institutionalize global civil society were made in the beginning of the twentieth century. The ultimate effort being the protection of the interest of the disadvantaged sections of people of the backward regions thereby enabling them to object against the exploitation of one country by another. 'The creation of central office of International Association founded in 1907 by Nobel Laureate Henri La Fontaine (1907) which was later on renamed as the Union of International Association is a major step towards achieving the above goals i.e. linking together the non-governmental groups working in different parts of the world. The first half of the twentieth century witnessed the creation of NGO coalitions to advocate on specific issues such as the international women's association, labour unions and associations for the promotion of world peace. Soon, it was evident that the non-governmental organization sector began to fill the vacuum left by both the corporate sector and the nation states in international relief and development activities. Venkataiah, (2009). The role of the NGOs is extremely significant with regard to global governance. This can be proved by the fact that the position of some NGOs like Amnesty International, Red Cross, Green Peace and World Women Federation (WWF) are much more powerful both in terms of staff and financial position than some international organizations such as the U.N., Human Rights Commission, WTO, UNCTAD and UNIDO.

4.6 NON-GOVERNMENTAL ORGANIZATIONS IN THE INDIAN SCENARIO

Since the end of the Second World War, the developing countries have witnessed an enormous economic and political turmoil characterized by a remarkable economic growth rate followed by a complete failure in the provision of distributive justice to the vast majority of population especially the rural poor. Bongartz, (1970). The chief characteristic feature of most of the developing countries happened to be rampant poverty, illiteracy, mal-nutrition and high mortality rate in spite of the existence of developmental programmes for improving the situation. 'This has given momentum to search for more adequate and appropriate strategies for improving the living conditions of the poor population and started a good deal of discussion about the systematic alternative development strategies, such as the integrated development approach; the basic needs approach, community participation, self-help and self-reliance concept.' Ravishankar, (2003). Such concepts, approaches and strategies constitute the basic element behind the large scale development of development in the number of NGOs around the globe highlighting on people centred developmental agenda for bringing about justice, sustainability and self-reliance.

During the 1990's when India adopted the policy of Liberalisation, Privatisation and Globalisation (LPG), the balance of payment crisis happened to be the major reason behind it. In such a situation, the importance of the non-governmental organizations began to grow because of the shift in the focus from the traditional 'trickle down approach of the bureaucracy to the people centred participatory approach along with human development and economic growth (UN, Human Development Report, 1993)'. Ramesh K Arora (2001) prefers to visualize this changed conceptualization of government system as that where the significance of the people have moved to the centre from the periphery. 'Thus, in the era of globalization, people centred governance depends increasingly on Community Based Organisations (CBOs), Non-Governmental Organisations (NGOs), Voluntary Bodies, Local Self-Governance Institutions, Castes, Religious and Ethnic Association and other Civil Society Organisations'. Arora (2001). According to the World Bank Report 2000-2001, 'the NGOs shows the poor people how to make a difference if they are organized themselves to defend their rights to take advantage of market opportunities and protect themselves from risks'. World Encyclopaedia, (2015).

4.7 RISE IN THE NON-GOVERNMENTAL ORGANIZATIONS

It is very difficult to estimate the exact number of NGOs operating in India because of a long tradition of voluntarism in the state. The different houses of registration furthermore complicate it because not all the NGOs are registered under one particular authority. They are spread in terms of registration under the Societies Act as NGOs, religious institutions like churches, sports associations, private hospitals, educational institutions and neighbourhood clubs not to forget the unregistered associations claiming themselves to be the torch bearers of social service in the society. According to Human Development Report, 2002, India had more than one million non-profit organizations. Dhabi, (2003). The major reason behind the emergence of the non-governmental organizations at such a massive scale signifies its importance in the contemporary society of India. There are some vital factors that have contributed to an increase in the number of NGO sector in India posing it to be an alternative strategy for social reform, change and transformation. Some of the noteworthy reasons for an increase in the growth of NGO sector in India can be listed as follows –

- Philanthropic attitude of people advocating on the lines of service to mankind as service to God, charity and goodness. Such idealistic commitments backed by humanitarian sentiments and religious values for the development of all especially the uncared people have led to a large scale growth in the number of the NGOs.

- The incorporation of industrialization, urbanization and in turn westernization has had a serious impact on the interest of the marginalized village craftsmen. The failure on the part of the governmental efforts in the direction of protecting the interests of these vulnerable groups has acted as a motivating factor for the NGOs to work for the upliftment of the former.

- It has been witnessed that the government has failed to protect the constitutional safeguards guaranteed to the people of the nation especially of the down trodden communities especially in areas of poverty, inequalities and social justice. This has called for an active involvement of the non-governmental organizations to work on the line of activism thereby empowering the weaker sections to demand for their rightful share from the state.

- With the advent of globalization, the market economy has failed to protect and meet the needs of the poor and the unorganized sections especially in the rural zones thereby leaving the platform open for the emergence and functioning of the non-governmental organizations.

- The implementation of the structural adjustment programmes thereby encouraging liberal economy with private enterprises has largely diminished the role of the state which has been reduced to mere regulator and facilitator of development – development being left to be considered as a collective effort of individuals, private sectors, public sector and non-governmental organizations.

- Lastly, the constant encouragement of the governmental policy especially in the implementation of Five-Year Plans for the working of the non-governmental organizations have led to a rise in the number of numbers of non-governmental sector in India. Venkataiah, (2009).

Thus, the above mentioned points may be regarded to be the chief reasons for the rise of the non-governmental organizations in the Indian soil.

4.8 ROLE OF THE NON-GOVERNMENTAL ORGANIZATIONS

With the change in the role of the government from a police state to a welfare state or a development state, it has been witnessed that the role played by the non-governmental organizations have also undergone serious changes from relief and charity to development and empowerment. Some of the major developmental roles played by the NGOs in the present day context of India has been summarized by Rai &Tandon (2008) as under –

- Planner and implementer of development programmes.
- Mobilization of local resources.
- Catalyst and innovator.
- Builder of self-reliant sustainable society.
- Mediator between people and government.
- Supporter and partner of government programmes in activating delivery system by implementing rural development programmes.

- Agent of demystifying technology.
- Facilitator of development in education, training, health etc.

The non-governmental organizations performed the above mentioned roles by motivating the people, mobilizing the resources, initiating leadership and by participating in development programmes for self-reliance. Prasad, (2008).

4.9 NON-GOVERNMENTAL ORGANISATIONS (NGOS) AND DEVELOPMENT

Although the tern NGO (non-governmental organization) may appear to be very simple yet one cannot overlook its largely scattered presence and capabilities in its definition. The non-governmental organizations provide us with an exorbitant range of organizations that vary in size, origin, ideology, programmes and the area of control thereby engulfing innumerable areas of work under its purview. Therefore, it can be stated that no standard definition can define a non-governmental organization but instead can only provide the chief characteristics of it working in different dimensions. Cernea (1988) believes that voluntarism in association is the key to all non-governmental organizations.

The World Bank defines the non-governmental organizations in terms of its basic characteristics in the following lines – "The diversity of NGOs strains any simple definition. They include many groups and institutions that are entirely or largely independent of government and that have primarily humanitarian or cooperative rather than commercial objectives. They are private agencies in industrial countries that support international development; indigenous groups organized regionally or nationally; and member-groups in villages. NGOs include charitable and religious associations that mobilize private funds for development, distribute food and family planning services and promote community organization. They also include independent cooperatives, community associations, water-user societies, women's groups and pastoral associations. Citizen Groups that raise awareness and influence policy are also NGOs".

The diverse activities of the non-governmental organizations makes it difficult for providing a single suitable definition in terms of defining them. Pokhrael (2000) believes the non-governmental organizations to be a welfare organization working in terms of voluntary services while Sundaram (1986) regard them to be the non-profit organizations that deal with the problems of the exploited and the poor people. Korten (2000) feels that the non-governmental organizations strive towards promotion of radical self organization at the individual level while Prabakarn (1992) defines it in terms of its structure that can be both: structured or unstructured, organized or unorganized. Bhose (2003) opines the non-governmental organizations to be a collective of the people that participate in the development process. Chand (1991) is of the view that the non-governmental organizations are both supplementary and complementary organizations created to deal with the diverse needs of the community. The operational definition of the NGOs sector adopted by Najam (2000) states that "NGOs includes the broad spectrum of voluntary associations that are entirely or largely independent and that are not primarily motivated by commercial concerns. These organizations are primarily motivated by the desire to articulate and actualize particular social vision and they operate in the realm of civil society through the shared normative values of their partner and clients".

Heinz (1989) states that the developing countries have experienced enormous political and economic change after the end of the Second World War where although successful industrialization in such third world countries were witness, it miserably failed in providing distributive justice especially to the majority population of the rural poor. With the decline in the role of the state in social service and welfare programmes, the non-governmental organizations have increasingly gained attention and importance whereupon they are looked as an alternative agency in promoting development, change and awareness in the society. This however does not give us the license to underestimate the role of the State. Generally, the voluntary action group is known by the terms such as the non-governmental organizations, the voluntary organizations, the grassroot organizations and the action groups. The approach of the non-governmental organization towards the development of the people is based upon an important idea of people's participation without which development cannot be perceived. This approach is in sharp contrast to the top-down approach of the state where on the other hand the needs of the people are assigned topmost priority by considering the people not as objects but as subjects possessing the knowledge and ability to bring about change in the desired direction.

"The NGOs are the not-for-profit organizations that are independent of government and business and have been at the forefront of participatory development because their mode of operation places them in close contact with local communities. They are a response to a wide array of humanitarian, economic, social, political and environmental concerns, and consequently their aims and approaches are extremely diverse. NGOs also differ with regard to their respective stakeholders, resources and influence." Vakil (1997). It must be noted here that the role and functioning of the international NGOs termed as the INGOs with worldwide programmes such as Save the Children and Oxfam vary significantly in terms of their structure, funding and work pattern from the indigenous community level NGOs that function at the local level projects.

Since the early 1980s there has been witnessed a sharp increase in the number of the NGOs ranging from 1,700 in 1981 to 4000 in 1988. OECD (1988). The major reason behind the growth in the number and activities of the NGOs happened to be the financial difficulties confronting many southern countries in the 1980s and the rise in the number of fragile states followed by the complex emergencies of the 1990s.The end of the Cold War furthermore removed the military and ideological constraints enabling the intervention of the NGOs in humanitarian areas. Furthermore, due to the active participation of the media in the era of globalization, the plights of the poor people of the developing world have also pushed the NGOs to work in the required areas. The rise in the prominence of the NGOs can be witnessed from the fact that in the recent years, the various agencies of the UN and the World Bank have started religiously consulting with the NGOs in the process of policy formulation. 'In March 2009, there were 3172 NGOs in consultative status with the UN Economic and Social Council (ECOSOC), and some 400 NGOs accredited to the Commission on Sustainable Development (CSD), a subsidiary body of ECOSOC.'

Hopper (2012). The large scale incorporation of the NGOs in this manner is looked as a strategy of the World Bank to bring about participatory development from the mid 1990s onward. This was clearly evident in the fact that in more than 50% of the projects of World Bank of 1994, the NGOs were seen to be actively participating.

One of most important reasons behind the rise in the number and prominence of the NGOs is because it performs the function of *advocacy* especially for those who fail to express their opinion in the power relation structure. Generally, the NGOs work towards lobbying, campaigning, education and policy research as an attempt to bring about humanitarian and development awareness amongst all. "In particular, NGOs seek to influence public opinion, governments and IGOs on issues like debt relief, child labour, the nature of international trade and human rights based agendas and approaches by development NGOs." Nelson and Dorsey (2008). Those NGOs that are oriented towards advocacy seek to develop the position of the world's poor by challenging the international economic and political structures that contribute to their subjugation. However, scholars like Edward and Hulme in 1992 criticized the NGOs for not being able to provide an alternative to the existing system and of only complaining about the present condition.

In closely analysing the role and functioning of the NGOs one can opine that the neo liberals stand positive about the existence of the NGOs because according to them, the NGOs and other voluntary organizations are locally oriented which brings them in a better position to understand and deal with the local problems. The critics of neo liberalism on the other hand believe that the NGOs behave in the manner in which their donor agencies want them to behave therefore leaving no scope for addressing the grass root problem of the people. In defending the position of the NGOs some supporters argue that they serve multiple purposes like filling in of the gap of social welfare which the state may at times fail to address, tackle poverty through food distribution, provides training and education and credit in the form of micro credit facilities.

The non-governmental organizations are dependent and influenced by the State, national and international funds and other socio-political environmental factors which in the long run paint them in terms of their ideology of development as well as fund raising programmes; but at the same time, it tries its level best to cling on to participation of the people for development. The direct impact of globalization and liberalization has posed a serious threat to the livelihood, culture and eco-system by the market forces of the West that ultimately aim to bring about homogenization of the diverse cultures. In such a situation the non-governmental organizations can mediate between the State, the Multi-National Corporations, the International Organisations such as the WTO and the World Bank by acting as a buffer and protector in between.

4.10 SITUATING THE NGOS IN INDIA

In the Indian context, the origin and the functioning of the NGOs is slightly different which has been briefly outlined below.

India has a long history of civil society based on the concepts of daana (giving) and seva (service). Voluntary organizations — organizations that are voluntary in spirit and without profit-making objectives — were active in cultural promotion, education, health, and natural disaster relief as early as the medieval era. They proliferated during British rule, working to improve social welfare and literacy and pursuing relief projects. During the second half of the 19th century, nationalist consciousness spread across India and self-help emerged as the primary focus of sociopolitical movements. Numerous organizations were established during this period, including the Friend-in-Need Society (1858), Prathana Samaj (1864), Satya Shodhan Samaj (1873), Arya Samaj (1875), the National Council for Women in India (1875), and the Indian National Conference (1887). The Societies Registration Act (SRA) was approved in 1860 to confirm the legal status of the growing body of non-governmental organizations (NGOs). The SRA continues to be relevant legislation for NGOs in India, although most state governments have enacted amendments to the original version. Christian missionaries active in India at this time directed their efforts toward reducing poverty and constructing hospitals, schools, roads, and other infrastructure.

Mahatma Gandhi's return to India in 1916 shifted the focus of development activities to economic self-sufficiency. His Swadeshi movement, which advocated economic self-sufficiency through small-scale local production, swept through the country. (Asian Development Bank).

The non-governmental organizations in India portray a wide range of diversity in terms of their size, structure, funding, membership, philosophy, goals, programmes and most important of all their relationship with the political parties. The non-governmental organizations have been classified by eminent scholars in the following manner. Shah and Chaturvedi (1983) have classified the non-governmental organizations into i) techno-managerial NGO, ii) reformist NGO and iii) radical NGO. To Hirway

(1995), the NGOs are basically of three types namely, i) welfare oriented, ii) development organizations and iii) empowering NGOs. Korten (1990) has classified the NGOs into i) relief and welfare organizations, ii) coalitions building community organizations. Eliot (1987) believed that the NGOs can be categorized into i) charity, ii) development, iii) empowerment NGOs.

The policies and programmes of the non-governmental organizations point out the positive role that they play in the process of development. However, a critical analysis is very important to be drawn in order to draw a clear understanding about the role of the NGOs in fulfilling their duties in praxis.

4.11 NGOS AND TRIBAL DEVELOPMENT IN INDIA

The second quarter of the present century to the late seventies portrays an important pattern of tribal development that was adopted by both the official as well as the non-official agencies reflecting upon the existence of some weaknesses in different form and at different levels. The adoption of new patterns was considered to be necessary and this necessity changed its features with time. The ideology of various agencies were tested by time and often regarded to be faulty. Those voluntary organizations that preferred to work in complete isolation from the government in the process of tribal development were criticized but no concrete remedial measure was provided to address the situation. Monetary investments have been made at an alarming rate to bring about the desired development of the scheduled tribes which of course has not been successful enough in meeting the demands of the hour. The question of who is to be put to question – is it the State, is it the non-governmental organizations or is it the beneficiary scheduled tribes themselves, provides us with an interesting challenge to be resolved in the present volume. The problem of tribal development can be classified into two broad categories: the one which the tribals face, and the other which the functionaries working in the tribal society face. Both these categories occupy a place of significance because without addressing the two, the conclusion drawn would be at fault. The research work shall address the problem of tribal development from both the angles. However, in doing so, the heterogeneous components of the scheduled tribes shall definitely pose a problem as well as a variation in addressing this issue.

It cannot be denied that social development is the primary duty of the state, however in the developing countries which are marked by the limitation of state and expansion of the NGO sectors, efficiency is expected more from the later. The state is believed to create an environment for development while the NGOs are entrusted to implement the development agenda of the government amongst the grassroots in an economic and efficient manner. At times, the non-governmental organizations are also seen working in close collaboration with the state mechanism as partners in achieving the target of development.

The development of the scheduled tribes cannot be visualized without an active support and an efficient role of the non-governmental organizations in close collaboration with the sincere efforts of the government. This is because one of the prominent reasons behind the underdevelopment of the scheduled tribes happens to be their isolated geographical habitation characterized by hills, forests, river beds and untraceable geographical locations.

The case studies conducted in the research work proves the fact that the government officials hesitate to settle down in those areas and work for the development of the needy scheduled tribe communities. They demand for immediate transfers and some even go to the extent of resigning from their prestigious post and thereby leaving the office empty. Interestingly, the head of the government honourable Prime Minister portrays his awareness about this issue which is why in his lecture in the seminar conducted at the parliament he makes it an attempt to remove the misconception of punishment postings and translates it as an opportunity to serve the fellow countrymen. (*We for Development*, 2018).

In such a situation, the role of the non-governmental organizations stands to be crucial in addressing the immediate needs of the tribal population. Several surveys have been conducted that testifies the fact that the scheduled tribe communities largely believe the non-governmental organizations can perform their duties in a much better manner only if they are genuinely serious about their jobs. This puts a question mark to the integrity of the non-governmental organizations working in the area of tribal development. Those tribal areas that have honest non-governmental organizations working in the area have definitely shown a better quality of life as compared to those where the non-governmental organizations exist only for namesake. Moreover, the attitude and approach of the non-governmental organizations towards the beneficiary scheduled tribes generally plays an important role in their overall development because grassroot friendly approaches seen to be the need of the hour which needs to be clearly understood by the non-governmental organizations.

The idea of development as we have studied in our earlier sections is a reflection of the understanding of development from the view point of the government, the academicians, the external agencies and any such organs that have assumed to conceptualize it from above not being a member to its impact. The voices of the marginalized have always been neglected and unheard which has resulted in the creation of a huge gap in the idea of development understood by the external agencies on the one hand, and that which is interpreted by the beneficiaries themselves on the other hand. This is because there has not taken place a required amount of consultation of the beneficiaries taking them into confidence by the policy framers thereby resulting in the mismatched idea of development which fail to address the needs of the scheduled tribes and in turn widen the gap between the two.

Therefore, it can be safely stated that the alternative agencies of tribal development like the non-governmental organisations, the voluntary organisations, the civil society and the like cannot be undermined because development through a holistic approach is extremely important. As has been stated earlier the structure, organisation and vision of such agencies make it more reliable, people friendly and change oriented for the targets of tribal development to be achieved swiftly. Having said so the aspect of accountability can not be underrated because a large number of cases have been reported where fake organisations have mushroomed in and spoiled the very objective of decentralisation. Therefore, checks and balances should be introduced without complicating the procedure whereby the beneficiaries must be integrated for achieving the desired output.

Bibliography

Abraham M, George. (2004). *"India Untouched: The Forgotten Face of Rural Poverty"*. Madras: East West Books Pvt. Ltd.

Aguirre, D. (2011). *The Human Right to Development in a Globalised World*. England: Ashgate Publishing Limited.

Allen, T., & Allan, T. (2000). *Poverty and Development into the 21st Century*. UK: Oxford University Press.

Anand, S., & Sen, A. (2000). Human Development and Economic Sustainability. *World Development*, 28(12): 2029-2049.

Barnett, H. G. (1953). *Innovation: the Basis of Culture Change*. New York: McGraw Hill.

Barnett, T. (1989). *Social and Economic Development*. New York: Guilford Press.

Bauer, P. T. (1981). *Equality, the Third World and Economic Delusion*. London: Methuen.

Bhowmik, P. K. (1987). "Development and Anthropology: Rebuilding Rural and Tribal Economy', in *Anthropology, Development and Nation Building*, ed. by A. K. Kalla and K. S. Singh. New Delhi: Concept Publishing Company.

Bijoy, C. R., Gopalakrishnan, S., & Khanna, S. (2010). *India and the Rights of Indigenous Peoples*. AIPP.

Brohman, J. (1996). *Popular Development Rethinking the Theory and Practice of Development*. UK: Blackwell.

Burman, B. K. R. (1994). *Tribes in Perspective*. Delhi: Mittal Publications.

Cardoso, F., & Faleto, R. (1979). *Dependency and Development*. Berkley and Los Angeles: University of California Press.

Cernea, M. (1988). 'Non-Governmental Organisations and Local *Development' World Bank Discussion Papers.*Washington D.C.: World Bank.

Chambers, R. (1997). *Whose reality counts?: Putting the First Last.* London: Intermediate Technology Publication Ltd.

Chandra, S. (2001). *Non-Governmental Organisations: Structure, Relevance and Function.* New Delhi: Kanishka Publishers, Distributors.

Chattopadhyay, K. (1978). *Tribalism in India.* New Delhi: Humanities Pr.

Chaudhuri, S. K. (2004). *Constraints of Tribal Development.* New Delhi: Mittal Publications.

Chaudhuri, S. N. (2004). *Dalit and Tribal Leadership in Panchayats.* New Delhi: Concept Publishing Company.

Cox, D. R., & Pawar, M. (2012). *International Social Work: Issues Strategies and Programmes.* New Delhi: Sage Publications.

Danda, A. K. (1991.) *Tribal Economy in India.* New Delhi: Inter- India Publications.

Danda, Ajit Kr. (1993). 'A Plea for Political Mobility' in M. Miri (ed.) *Continuity and Change in Tribal Society.* Shimla: Indian Institute of Advanced Study.Dar, S. U. (1992). *Impact of Integrated Rural Development Programme.* New Delhi: Anmol Publications.

David, B. L., & David, C. K. (1989). *Understanding the Voluntary Organizations.* Washington DC: The World Bank.

David, L., & Wallace, T. (Ed.). (2003). *"Development NGOs and the Challenge of Change: New Roles and Relevance".* New Delhi: Rawat Publications.

Elwin, V. (1959). *A Philosophy for NEFA.* Shillong: The Advisor to Governor of Assam.

Escobar, A. (1995). *Encountering Development: the Making and Unmaking of the Third World*. Princeton: Princeton University Press.

Ferguson, J. (1990). *The Anti-politics Machine.Development, Depoliticization and Bureaucratic Power in Lesotho*. Cambridge: Cambridge University Press.

Foucault, M. (1972). *The Archaeology of Knowledge*. Trans. A. M. Sheridan Smith. New York: Harper & Row.

Giddens, A. (1979). *Central Problems in Social Theory: Action, structure and contradiction in social analysis*. London: The Macmillan Press Ltd.

Giddens, A. (1984). *The constitution of society: Outline of the theory of structuration*. Cambridge: Polity Press.

Goel, O. P. (2004). *Role of NGOS in Development of Social System*. Gujarat: ISHA Books.

Goodland, R. (1985). 'Tribal People and Economic Development: The Human Ecological Dimension' in Jeffery A. Macneely and David Pitt, eds., *Culture and Consevation: The Human Dimension in Environmental Planning*, Londa, Croom helm, pp. 13-30.

Hume, D. (ed.). (1987). *Essays, Moral, Political and Literary*. Indianapolis: University of Indiana Press.

Innes, S. (1995). *Creating the Commonwealth: The Economic Culture of Puritan New England*. New York: Norton.

Jean, D., & Sen, A. (2002). *India: Development and Participation*. Delhi: Oxford University Press.

Korten, D. (1992). *Getting to the 21st Century: Voluntary Action and the Global Agenda*. New Delhi: Oxford and IBH.

Kosambi, D. D. (1975). *The Culture and Civilization of Ancient India in Historical Outline*. Delhi: Vikas Publishing House.

Kothari, R. (1981). *State Against Democracy: In Search of a Humane World Order*. Delhi: Ajanta Publications.

Mishra, S. N., Sharma, K., & Sharma, N. (1984). Participation and Development. New Delhi: N.B.O. Publishers.

Mohanty, S., & B. M. Jena. (1991). 'Barriers to Educational Development among the Tribals' in H. C. Upadhyay (ed.), *Scheduled Castes and Scheduled Tribes in India*. New Delhi: Anmol Publications.

Pathy, J. (1992). 'The Idea of Tribe and the Indian Scene', in *Tribal Transformation in India*, Vol. 3, edited by Buddhadeb Chaudhuri. New Delhi: Inter-India Publications.

Rath, G. C. (ed.). (2006). *Tribal Development in India: The Contemporary Debate*. New Delhi: Sage Publications.

Rathnaiah, E. V. (1977). *Structural Constraints in Tribal Education*. New Delhi: Sterling Publishers Pvt. Ltd.

Sinha, Surajit. (1987). *Tribal Polities and State Systems in Pre-colonial Eastern and North Eastern Indian*. Calcutta: Centre for Studies in Social Sciences and K. P. Bagchi & Co.

Smith, C., & Freedman, A. (1972). *Voluntary Associations: Perspectives on the Literature*. London: Havard University Press.

Xaxa, V. (2008). *State, Society, and Tribes: Issues in Post-Colonial India*. New Delhi: Dorling Kindersley (India) Pvt. Ltd.

www.ingramcontent.com/pod-product-compliance
Lightning Source LLC
La Vergne TN
LVHW091321150826
845673LV00006B/1717

* 9 7 9 8 8 9 6 9 9 1 0 7 6 *